Mountain Bike Magic

Mountain Bike Magic

Rob van der Plas

Drawings by
Dan Cooney
Jim Zarka
Rob van der Plas
Photos
as credited

Bicycle Books

Copyright:	© 1991, Rob van der Plas
	Printed in Singapore
	First printing, 1991

Published by:	Bicycle Books, Inc.
	PO Box 2038
	Mill Valley CA 94941
	USA

Distributed to the book trade by: USA: The Talman Company, New York NY
Canada: Raincoast Book Distribution, Vancouver BC
Great Britain: Chris Lloyd Sales and Marketing Services, Poole, Dorset

| Cover and book design: | Dan Cooney, Cooney & Garfield |

| Cover photograph: | Gene Anthony |

| Frontispiece photograph: | Gordon Bainbridge |
| | Along the route of the Pearl Pass Tour near Crested Butte, Colorado. |

Cataloging in Publication Data: Van der Plas, Robert, 1938 —
Mountain Bike Magic. Bibliography: p. Includes Index.
1. Bicycles and bicycling — manuals, handbooks, etc.
2. Mountains, recreational use.
3. Authorship
I. Title
Library of Congress Catalog Number 91-71167
ISBN: 0-933201-41-9

About the Author

ROB VAN DER PLAS was the first author to devote a book specifically to the mountain bike and its use. Published March 1984 and regularly updated since then, his *Mountain Bike Book* is today still the ultimate technical manual on the mountain bike and the sport of off-road cycling. Mountain Bike Magic is his second book about the subject.

An engineer and writer by trade, and an experienced off-road cyclist himself, he has spent much of the last 15 years working on bicycle related projects. During that time, he has written over a dozen books and scores of articles for specialist periodicals on both sides of the Atlantic.

Growing up in Holland and England, he used the bicycle on unpaved roads many years before the idea of the mountain bike matured. Once it had, he immediately took to this fat-tire miracle. Today, he is a full-time writer and lives on the slopes of Mount Tamalpais in California's Marin County, the very place where the mountain bike was born.

"He immediately took to the mountain bike."

Gene Anthony photograph, taken in the Marin Headlands, California.

Author's Preface

THE MOUNTAIN BIKE has come of age. Grown out of the clunkers used by the daredevil downhill riders of California and Colorado in the late seventies, and first produced commercially in the early eighties, it is now the bike of fashion. And a sensible fashion it is: Unlike the ten-speeds of the seventies, which mostly rusted away in basements and garages across the land because most people never felt comfortable on them, mountain bikes beg to be used. Comfortable and safe, practical and enjoyable, the mountain bike is the bicycle of the future. And with increasing motor traffic pressure on the roads, off-road is the way to go.

This book sums up the state of the art. Rather than wasting the reader's time repeating the oft told story of the bike's emergence and the tall tales of the pioneers, it simply and clearly shows how to choose a bike and components from the range of equipment available today. And rather than copying the rules of off-road cycling organizations and race organizers, it tells you how to make the bike do what you want it to. And where words fail, the illustrations take over to reinforce the message — the book is illustrated in full color with beautiful photographs and clear drawings.

"The mountain bike is the bicycle of the future."

As with all other books published by Bicycle Books, this book is written to be useful to both the North American and the British market. Consequently, there will be some instances where terms are 'doubled up,' so as to make make it unambiguoues to both American and British readers. Other than that, American spelling is adhered to — with apologies to those who find it hard to accept *tyre* spelt *tire*, *aluminium* without the second *i*, and *pedalling* with only one *l*.

Finally, I should point out that in an effort to keep the language simple and easy to understand, I have compromised my unabated support for the equality of the sexes. Thus, the masculine form will generally be used when addressing the reader, rather than confusing the issue with too many he/she, him/her and *-person* constructions. The author and his editor believe it makes for a more readable book.

Table of Contents

Chapter 1
Mountain Biking Today . 9

Characteristics of Today's Mountain Bike 10
Mountain Biking Defined 12
Trail Access 12
Mountain Biking as a Sport 16
Mountain Bike Fashion 17

Chapter 2
Getting to Know the
Mountain Bike 19

The Parts of the Bike 21
The Frame 21
The Steering System 23
The Wheels 24
The Drivetrain 25
The Gearing System 26
The Brakes 27
Accessories 28

Chapter 3
Using the Gears 29

The Parts of the Gearing System 30
Index Derailleurs 30
The Rear Derailleur 31
The Front Derailleur 32
Derailleur Controls 33
Gearing Theory 33
Gear Designation 35
The Gear Progression 36
Gearing Practice 37

Chapter 4
Basic Riding Skills 39

Sizing the Bike to the Rider 40
Steering and Balancing 42
Braking 44
Starting and Accelerating 47
Climbing 47
Descending 48

Chapter 5
Advanced Off-Road
Techniques 49

Rough-Surface Riding 49
Balancing the Bike 50
Getting Airborne 52
Taking Obstacles in Your Stride 55
Overcoming Depressions 57

Chapter 6
Equipment and
Accessories 59

Protection 59
Mountain Bike Clothing 61
Mountain Bike Accessories 63

Chapter 7
Health and Safety . . . 67
The Risks of Mountain Biking 67
Off-Road 'Traffic' Hazards 68
Falls and Collisions 69
Treating Injuries 72
Other Health Problems 73

Chapter 8
Keeping Fit — On and Off
the Bike 77
Aerobic Fitness 78
Fit to Ride 79
Calisthenics and Stretching 80
Breathing Exercises 82
Wind Load Simulator Training 84
Massage 85

Chapter 9
Getting the Most out of
Your Bike 87
Prepare for the Weather 88
Rough Weather Wear 89
Other Equipment 91
Riding Style 92
Using the Mountain Bike for Transportation 94

Chapter 10
Mountain Bike Touring . 95
Choice of Equipment 96
Packing the Load 97
Planning the Tour 98
Executing the Tour 101

Chapter 11
Mountain Biking for
Competition 103
Types of Races 106
Equipment 106
Training for Off-Road Racing 108

Chapter 12
Maintaining the Mountain
Bike 111
Quick-Release Operation 112
Cleaning the Bike 112
Inspection and Lubrication 113
Maintenance 114
Brake Maintenance 114
Derailleur Maintenance 115
Drivetrain Maintenance 116
Wheel Maintenance 117
Bearing Adjustment 121
Handlebar Adjustment 121
Saddle Adjustment 122
Pedal Removal and Installation 122

Appendix 123
Table 1 — Gearing table 123
Table 2 — Metric gearing table 123
Table 3 — Frame sizing table 124
Index 125

CHAPTER 1

Mountain Biking Today

"In less than ten years, the mountain bike has become the mainstay of the bicycle industry and the most popular bike ever."

THESE DAYS, mountain biking is where it's at. In the United States, more than 70 percent of all adult bicycles sold in the last few years have been mountain bikes, and the trend is rapidly gaining momentum in most other countries too. In less than ten years, the mountain bike has become the mainstay of the bicycle industry and the most popular bike ever.

It's no wonder either, because the mountain bike is the first bicycle development to bring improvements both to the experienced cyclist and to those who formerly did not think of themselves as cyclists — those millions who had at best bought whatever bike was in fashion before, but never really took to riding it. The mountain bike allows the experienced cyclist to do things he had hardly dreamed of before, and it allows those who did not take to cycling before to enjoy the sport and the machine for the first time.

Mountain biking near Lake Tahoe, about 7,500 ft above sea level.
Gordon Bainbridge photo.

Characteristics of Today's Mountain Bike

"Individual bike designs vary, depending on what kind of use they are designed for."

Since the mountain bike was first commercially made available in the early eighties, quite a few refinements have been introduced, and most of these make off-road cycling easier — making the mountain bike more suitable as the universal bike for all purposes. Of course, individual bike designs vary, depending on what kind of use they are designed for, from downhill bombers to agile climbers and from long distance touring bikes to trials machines for riding slowly in the most challenging terrain. Nevertheless, there is a clear trend and most mountain bikes now have quite a number of features in common. In Chapter 2, the technical details of the mountain bike will be discussed more thoroughly, but here are some of the points that reflect the evolution of the mountain bike to its present state.

The most characteristic feature of all mountain bikes remains the use of fat tires that — unlike those of the old utility bike — are light and flexible. They are designed in such a way that they can withstand significant pressures to minimize rolling resistance when the surface is smooth, while also providing cushioning on uneven surfaces and traction on loose ground. For real off-road use, the fatter the better, and the size designation 26 x 2.125 or bigger seems the way to go except for those who really don't intend to ride off-road (nothing wrong with that: the mountain bike has enough advantages on the road to justify its use there for most cyclists).

The next most common feature is the handlebar design, which is, though still generally flat and straight, now relatively narrow (typically about 22 inches), with ends that are angled for a more ergonomic grip. The handlebars are mounted on an adjustable stem so they can be turned into the most comfortable position and the stem can be interchanged to bring the bars closer or further away as it suits the rider's body proportions.

The seat, or saddle, is no longer always mounted with a quick-release, although most are. In practice, few riders ever change the height of their saddles, and since quick-releases only add weight, while encouraging theft or vandalism, it is not always necessary to have one. And those saddles themselves are getting more sophisti-

Mountain bike with suspension.

"Skilled riders tend to prefer conventional over-the-bar shifters, that can be shifted over several steps."

cated all the time, now often using a gel material that takes on the shape of the rider's contact surface — even though this writer still prefers to use an 'old fashioned' English leather saddle with coil springs in the back.

All mountain bikes have derailleur gearing, and nothing primitive: most come with 21 speed systems and all are indexed, so shifting from one gear to the next is always precise, without the awkward fidgeting that frustrated so many would-be cyclists only five or six years ago. Entry-level bikes usually have under-the-bar shifters that are simply pushed in once to get into the next higher or lower gear, whereas more skilled riders tend to prefer conventional over-the-bar thumb shifters that can be shifted over several steps, although at the price of releasing their grip somewhat.

The brakes are now once more the way they were in the beginning: After some experimenting with other designs, now virtually all mountain bikes use so-called cantilever brakes, which themselves have also evolved to the point where they no longer project from the bike the way the early models did. Some of them have return springs in the brake levers to make braking even lighter.

In this connection it is necessary to point out that at least Shimano, the industry's major component manufacturer, has integrated braking and gearing components to the point where they work perfectly — but lock the rider into equipment that does not allow individual exchanges (and who wants to throw away his entire braking-and-gearing system, when only one part is damaged?). Some other manufacturers have managed to produce equally good equipment without integrating the kitchen sink.

Two types of mountain bike. Left, a high-end Ritchey mountain bike. Right, Nishiki's original version of Richard Cunningham's raised chainstay design.

Various tire profiles for different kinds of terrain.

Mountain Biking Defined

If one is to attempt to define mountain biking, it might seem obvious to refer to cycling in the mountains, and indeed that is more or less the way the sport started out. Today, however, it would seem fairer to define it very loosely as any kind of riding using a mountain bike. Since many mountain bikes are rarely used off-road, the most that can be said is that it is the use of a bike that is suitable for extensive off-road use.

And what is off-road, anyway? I used to think it means cross-country, but that is certainly at best frowned upon in most parts of the world, because environmental concerns speak against riding where nobody has gone before: This world is messed up enough without every crazy cyclist drawing his own tracks to erode what little nature is left. So *off-road* means *on trail.* Those trails are not open to regular motor vehicle traffic, and they may be unpaved or improved with anything short of a sealed asphalt surface. In fact, where I grew up, as well as many other parts of the world, there are plenty of regular roads that are rougher than some of the trails that see no more than the occasional ranger's truck in the US.

The charm of mountain biking actually lies in the loose definition, because it is the ability to ride off-road as well as on regular roads, in the mountains as well as on level ground, in the country as well as in the city, that makes the sport so practical and enjoyable. No need to drive out to the trail head in a car. That's the problem with hiking: Most trails start so far from urban areas or public transportation terminals that a few miles of hiking invariably calls for a considerable distance driven in a car. Not my idea of getting back to nature or displaying environmental concern, and easy to avoid with the mountain bike, even if you don't live right around the corner from a mountain biking paradise.

"This world is messed up enough without every crazy cyclist drawing his own tracks."

Trail Access

One thing has not exactly improved since the mountain bike was first introduced. Unfortunately for us, there is increasing resistance to the idea of allowing bicycle access to existing suitable trails. From the fire roads of

Mixed use: Mountain bikers and equestrians, yes even hikers, can share the open space, and there is no need for the proliferation of 'no cycling' signs.
Photos by Gene Anthony (top) and Gordon Bainbridge (below).

Mountain bike components have reached the stage of art, as this Campagnolo brake detail testifies.

Mount Tamalpais in California to the footpaths of Zermatt in Switzerland, the fight for access has been a losing battle for mountain bikers in recent years, and it's time to fight back.

A case in point is taking place right at my doorstep. When I first settled in San Francisco back in the early seventies, I used to take my bicycle across the Golden Gate Bridge and ride on the unpaved trails of the Marin Headlands, at that time public land under the control of the military, and since then integrated into something called the Golden Gate National Recreational Area. At the time (note this was well before the first mountain bike was developed and I rode an ordinary ten-speed), nobody objected. I met the occasional hiker and a few other cyclist, and we didn't have any conflicts Of course, mountain bikers can share the outdoors with others too.

Today, even though the area is now specifically designated for recreational use, as opposed to conservation, where one could understand some resistance to increased public use, hikers, horsemen and administrators are hand-in-hand waging war against the mountain bikers. The hearings on the subject are attended by many more cyclists than hikers and equestrians, accurately reflecting the amount of use for those groups respectively. But the climate is very much anti-cycling. A staff member was given the assignment to investigate the relationship between cycling and erosion and fell right into the *post hoc ergo procter hoc* fallacy. Merelely finding erosion and cyclists in the same place does not suffice mean cycling is causing the erosion, but that is the argument that was used to close down most of the trails to mountain bikers, much to the hikers' delight.

So now cycling is only permitted where specifically posted. Off course, that is the wrong way round: just neglecting to put up a sign, or even vandalizing one, should not make cycling illegal where it causes no problem. Single-track trails (i.e. those not wide enough for a pick-up truck) had already been declared off-limits to cyclists before. The only legal places to ride now are a few of the wide trails that run from the main road to one picnic ground or another — no loops, no connecting trails, no narrow, challenging rides.

A few miles to the north the Marin Municipal Water District, with generous funding from the equestrians, enforces restrictions with respect to speed, time of day and

You don't have to be sane to ride a mountain bike.
Anders Lewendal shows how easy it is to do
something exciting. He did borrow someone else's
bike for the occasion though — just in case.
Gordon Bainbridge photos.

Mountain bike racer Jacquie Phelan, riding her Charles Cunningham aluminum bike. Gordon Bainbridge photo.

access with radar traps and draconic fines of $200 or more. All that for no good reason, because the mountain bike can easily be ridden safely and congenially, even at speed.

Mountain Biking as a Sport

Very shortly after the first mountain bikes became commercially available, officially sponsored competition was started. Well, 'officially' is a big word: In keeping with the laid-back attitude of the early mountain bikers on the West Coast, NORBA, the National Off-Road Bicycling Association, was hardly very rigidly organized. So much so, in fact, that the original directors saw fit to sell the organization to one of their number just to be relieved of the hassle. The organization changed hands a few more times, and finally ended up being taken over by what had originally been the competition, namely the United States Cycling Federation, the very organization that had at first done all in its power to strangle the upstart sport of mountain biking. Nowadays the USCF lets the mountain bikers within their organization do pretty much what they want, living proof of the fact how mountain biking can't be forced into some strict mould.

Actually, mountain bike racing dates back to the very origins of the mountain bike. As early as 1978 unofficial off-road races were held on converted utility bikes, referred to as clunkers. These races were invariably downhill challenges, but with time the challenge of riding uphill became as important as the downhill suicide trip. Today's mountain bikes actually come in different designs, some of them being better suited for downhill use (these now often have some kind of suspension), others for uphill riding. And in the Northwest, as well as in New England, an entirely different form of competition is popular. Called *trials*, or *observed trials*, it is not a battle of speed but purely of skills, the idea being to ride over impossible obstacles without getting off the bike. And you guessed it, special bikes (with high bottom brackets, small wheels and small frames) are available for this discipline too.

Personally, I like to have a bike for all uses — a universal bike. I don't need to be the fastest downhill, nor the toughest uphill or the cleverest trials rider. Just give me a bike that will go uphill and down, on good roads and on difficult passages. And, believe it or not, there is such a bike. Every regular mountain bike will do all these things admirably well.

Mountain Bike Fashion

There is such as thing as fashion in mountain biking. Not only are the bikes themselves offered in ever more different colors and designs, also the clothing for their users and the gadget intended for their bikes have gone through a minor revolution since the early days. Cut-off blue jeans and T-shirts may have been the garb worn by the first mountain bikers, but certainly once the Europeans started mixing in, things have change.

Today, skin-tight lycra and spandex garments in futuristic colors are *en vogue* for the riders, and the earthy shades of the early mountain bikes have given way to the dazzling painter's pallettes on wheels some manufacturers display. And the color schemes change each

No, this photo was not taken at a fashion show but at a European mountain bike race. Don't be fooled though: Those European racers are pretty tough and don't think anything of getting their colorful bikes and outfits covered with mud before the end of the race.
Andreas Schlüter photo.

Having fun on the mountain bike. Although you can't fly over the ground like this all the time, the thrill is always there.
This photo is copied from a publicity poster for Boulder Bicycles' full suspension Gazelle model — probably the best bike for doing things like this.

"Some changes are indeed nothing more than fashion statements that will go out of style as fast as they come in."

year, to make sure their fashion-crazed clients keep buying the latest.

It goes beyond the superficial, though. The design has changed too. Overall, frames have become shorter, yet the distance between saddle and handlebars has increased; frame angles (the angles of the tubes of the frame relative to each other) have become steeper; tires first got narrower, than thicker again, handlebars have become narrower and adjustable, aluminum often replaces steel, and the chainrings have gone from round to oval and back to round. Gear shifters and brakes have gone through some changes of their own.

Some of these changes are definite improvements, and they will be discussed in the chapters that follow. But some changes are indeed nohting more than fashion statements that will go out of style as fast as they come *in*. There is a useful moral to this story: You can often save yourself a bundle by choosing last year's model — perhaps it will be back *en vogue* a few years later.

CHAPTER 2

Getting to Know the Mountain Bike

"The mechanics of this machine are much more exposed and you will have to be familiar with their workings."

To do this kind of thing, the mountain bike has to be designed very ruggedly. Andreas Schlüter photo.

IN THIS CHAPTER, you will find just about anything you need to know to select the right type and quality of mountain bike and to be able to understand the most important technical aspects of the bike. After all, though the bicycle may not be as complicated as most other modern machines, it *is* a mechanical device. The fact that it is not as complex as a car or a sewing machine does not detract from the other side of the coin, namely that the mechanics of this particular machine are much more exposed and you will have to be familiar with their workings to do even the most basic maintenance on your bike.

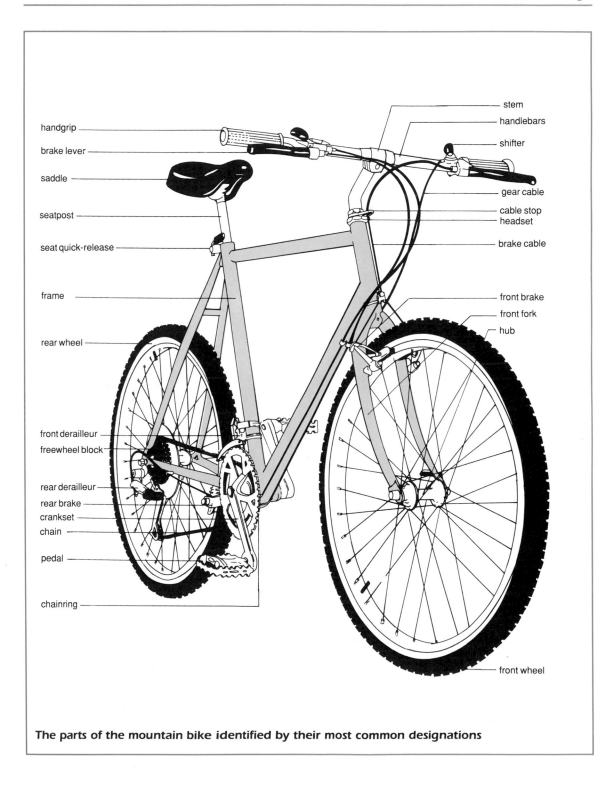

handgrip
brake lever
saddle
seatpost
seat quick-release
frame
rear wheel
front derailleur
freewheel block
rear derailleur
rear brake
crankset
chain
pedal
chainring

stem
handlebars
shifter
gear cable
cable stop
headset
brake cable
front brake
front fork
hub
front wheel

The parts of the mountain bike identified by their most common designations

Try the bike out for size before buying: Straddling the top tube, you should be able to lift the front wheel 5 or 6 inches. Gene Anthony photo.

The Parts of the Mountain Bike

The illustration on the facing page tells most of the story, but not all: It fails to convey how the many bits and pieces shown work and interact to operate as comprehensive systems. To make that clear, I will now walk you through the drawing, explaining what the various components are and what to look out for. First, by way of basic overview, it is best to separate out the various functional groups. In this vein, the following systems can be distinguished:

☐   frame

☐   steering system

☐   saddle and seatpost

☐   wheels

☐   drivetrain

☐   gearing system

☐   brakes

☐   accessories

Except for the accessories, which will be treated more thoroughly in Chapter 6, each of these groups will be described in detail in the sections that follow.

The Frame

Rightly referred to as the bicycle's backbone, this is of course the most important component of your mountain bike. It is generally the only part actually made by the manufacturer whose logo appears on the bike, and all the other components are mounted to it one way or another.

Even today, virtually all frames are built up of metal tubes in the familiar diamond shape. The front part, made up of large diameter tubes, is referred to as the *main frame*. The the rear portion made up of double, tubing is called the *rear triangle*. Although most frames are still built with steel tubing, the use of aluminum has rapidly increased in recent years, and even more exotic materials are in use: titanium, magnesium and epoxy-embedded carbon fiber (usually canned *composites*).

The difference between a mountain bike frame and that of a conventional drop-handlebar derailleur bike is

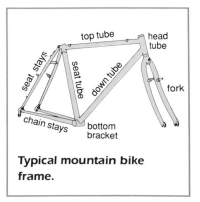

Typical mountain bike frame.

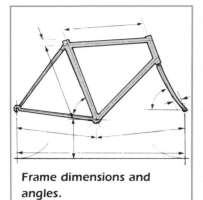

Frame dimensions and angles.

"Aluminum frames are not necessarily lighter than high-quality steel frames."

If you must have a woman's frame, make sure it looks like this, with additional rear stays connecting the rear drop-outs with the point where the top tube meets the seat tube.

mainly in the clearances for the (fatter) tires. In addition, mountain bikes are often made of thicker and slightly heavier-walled tubes to give the frame more strength and rigidity. For the latter reason, larger diameter tubes should preferably be used, especially when materials other than steel are selected, which are inherently less rigid (a slight increase in diameter makes a large difference to the rigidity).

Unlike regular bicycle frames, which are generally built by brazing the tubes together with lugs, most mountain bike frames are welded together using a relatively sophisticated welding process referred to as TIG (tungsten inert gas) welding. This allows the use of odd diameters and angles of the tubes relative to each other (lugs only come in standard sizes and angles) and playing such tricks as flaring or ovalizing the tubes locally.

Aluminum frames are not necessarily lighter than high-quality steel frames. The use of very strong steel alloys makes it possible to use very thin-walled tubes that are as light as aluminum tubes of the same strength. And even the high-tech solutions rarely lead to significant weight reductions relative to what can be achieved with high-quality steel tubes.

High-quality steel tubing is recognized by a label on one of the tubes, referring to double, triple or quadruple butted tubing made of e.g. chrome-moly steel. Both chrome-moly and manganese- molybdenum steel tubing can be extremely strong (yes, the buzz- word chrome-moly refers to nothing more than a steel alloy that is quite common, rather than some mystery metal, as some salespeople and add-textwriters imply).

As far as the design of mountain bike frames is concerned, apart from the greater diameters and wheel clearances, it should also have a higher bottom bracket (that's the location of the bearings for the cranks), so as to clear obstacles. To allow the rider to get close to the ground when necessary, mountain bike frames are typically some two inches smaller than conventional frames for the same rider. Smaller sizes should have sloping top tubes, so as to maximize the length of the headtube (the one that houses the bearings for the steering system) — needed to give the bike adequate stability. Finally, most good mountain bikes come with a variety of threaded bosses and eyelets for the installation of water bottles and luggage racks front and rear.

"In recent years, the mountain bike frame has seen a number of interesting developments."

In recent years, the mountain bike frame has seen a number of interesting developments that may or may not be the wave of the future. Quite a few frames are built with raised seat stays. This makes it possible to make the frame shorter, which is helpful in steep uphill situations, although it does tend to make the bike heavier. Another development is the use of suspension systems. Their advantage is that they keep the wheels on the ground, providing good steering and traction instead of just bouncing around. Especially for downhill riding, a lot is to be gained this way. But also on level ground there is a plus: as long as the ground is firm, the use of a suspension can offset tire cushioning. So you can inflate the tires to a higher pressure for less rolling resistance without sacrificing control or traction.

The Steering System

Both steering and balancing of a bicycle are achieved with the steering system, comprising front fork, handlebars, handlebar stem and the bearings of the headset. Although they work the same way as those of any other bike, there is a lot of difference relative to their counterparts on a ten-speed. The handlebars are almost straight, the stem usually raises them higher up (not a very clever thing to do, since the same effect is much better achieved with a longer head tube in the frame); and both fork and headset are nowadays often considerably beefier to make them more durable and increase steering precision and stability.

Foam handgrips are installed at the ends of the handlebars. The stem can be exchanged for one that brings

Mixed-use bikes.
Left, Hybrid bicycle with drop handlebars from Muddy Fox. Right, 'City-bikes' as supplied by Kuwahara for the European market.

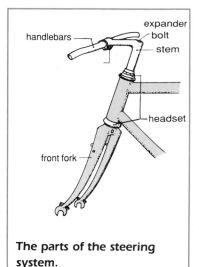

The parts of the steering system.

the handlebars closer (current fashion unfortunately stretches the distance between seat and handlebars too far for most riders and most conditions). The forks usually are welded up without a separate crown, referred to as unicrown forks. To be any good, they require reinforcement around the point where the two blades join the steerer tube, or fork shaft.

California mountain bike pioneer Koski introduced a very fine fork that is frequently used on high-end mountain bikes. It is beefed up to give optimum stability and strength, but with one infuriating feature: the fork-ends, or drop-outs, enclose the wheel attachments. Although thought of as a safety feature to prevent losing the front wheel, it completely defeats the purpose of the quick-release for wheel installation. When you have to remove and reinstall the wheel frequently, e.g. to transport the bike, you will soon get frustrated enough to grind those ridges down, as I did. Cheap bikes often have some other gizmo to trap the wheels, and there it is even more senseless, because those are the kind of bikes bought by people who don't ride much and if they do, they transport the bike in their car, removing and installing the wheel before and after every trip.

Typical front end detail. Gene Anthony photo.

The Wheels

Mountain bike wheels have come a long way since the days of the early clunkers. In fact, the wheel is where the greatest improvement has been, even though it is not the most visible. Modern wheels are light with strong but rather narrow aluminum rims, light and flexible high-pressure fat tires, and quick-release hubs. The narrow rims now used allow more of the tire to project in a nearly circular profile, giving ultimate cushioning and minimal rolling resistance.

Whereas early mountain bikes had solid axle hubs, which are theoretically stronger than equally dimensioned quick-release versions, modern quick-release hubs are at least as strong as the older variety with solid axles and axle nuts instead. On the other hand, quick-release hubs are not inherently better, just more convenient (providing you don't have the kind of gadget on the front fork described above to trap the wheel in place). Typically, mountain bike hubs are wider than

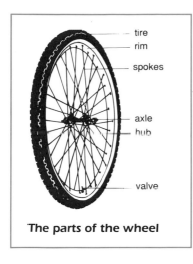

The parts of the wheel

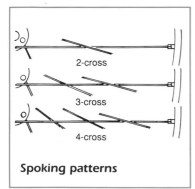

Spoking patterns

"Keep enough pressure to make sure the tires don't bottom out when riding over ridges."

those of racing bikes, as measured between the lock-nuts, giving the wheels more lateral stability.

It has also been found that the spokes don't necessarily have to be thicker, because their shorter length and the cushioning of the tire already protect them enough to withstand virtually all shocks even in the roughest terrain. The most common spoking patterns are shown in the illustration, and it is important to keep those spokes evenly and highly tensioned to prevent broken spokes and out-of-true wheels.

As far as tires are concerned, most mountain bikes still have tires and rims based on the dimensions of the American utility bike: 26 x 2.125 (referred to as 54-559 in the ISA international standard tire designation system). Whatever their width, they virtually all fit the same rims, the thicker tires just bulging out from the rim more than the skinnier ones. So-called hybrid bikes — mixed use machines based on the mountain bike — usually have narrower tires, and some of those actually use a different size rim, so it will be necessary to check for interchangeability in that case.

The tire tread patterns have evolved as well. Two trends can be distinguished: widely separated knobs for good grip on loose ground on the one hand, and lots of rubber with relatively few recesses (referred to as reverse pattern, and first introduced by racing tire specialist Continental). The inner tubes have become lighter and more flexible, because it has been found that the early thick, inflexible tubes deteriorate cushioning and rolling more than they aided puncture resistance.

Tire pressure is perhaps the most important variable. Keep it low (20–25 psi, or 1.3–1.7 bar) for adequate traction on very soft ground. Use higher pressures to minimize rolling resistance on harder ground; go all the way up to 70 or more psi (5 bar) for riding on smooth, hard surfaces. Whatever else, always keep enough pressure to make sure they don't bottom out when riding over ridges, to protect tubes, tires and rims.

The Drivetrain

Although often used to include the gearing system as well, I prefer to see this system as only the actual driven components: pedals, crankset, chain and freewheel

Above: Typical seat detail with quick-release binder bolt. Below: Not all mountain bikes have quick-releases, as this beautiful seat clamp detail on a Ritchey mountain bike demonstrates. Gene Anthony photos.

block. Here too, the trend has been away from the humongous stuff with which the early mountain bikes were equipped.

Today's mountain bike pedals are pretty sleek and light, and often come with nylon toeclips or even in patent clipless designs that attach directly to special shoes. The cranksets are no longer adaptations of touring or even racing designs, but have been specially designed for mountain bike use. If off-round chainrings are used at all anymore (they were all the craze just a few years ago), then only on the two smaller chainrings used for low-speed climbing. The bottom bracket is typically wider than on a racing bike, with the bearings as far out as possible, which is good engineering practice. Sealed bearing units are preferred by some, whereas the argument in favor of adjustable bearing units is that it is easy to take them apart for maintenance.

Some years ago, Shimano introduced special tooth designs for both the front chainrings and the rear sprockets on the freewheel, referred to as Superglide and Hyperglide respectively, and these also call for the use of special chains to match them. Most chains work well on all other chainrings, but some riders report difficulties shifting gears with particular combinations, so it is best to enquire at the bike shop which chain is suitable for use with the components on your bike.

The Gearing System

Mountain bikes have derailleur gearing, and its use will be outlined in some detail in Chapter 3. Generally, three chainrings in the front are combined with six or seven sprockets on the rear, resulting in a theoretical choice of 18 or 21 gears, respectively. Although there is so much overlap that you generally have only about 10 really different gears, the theoretical number is the one used.

Mountain bike derailleurs and shifters have evolved significantly, but they are still installed roughly where they used tobe, and they still work pretty much the same. They *are* a lot easier to use, and that has been the secret to the mountain bike's unexpected success worldwide. Mostly shifters, derailleurs and cables must be bought to match each other, because the indexed systems are quite sensitive to mismatching problems.

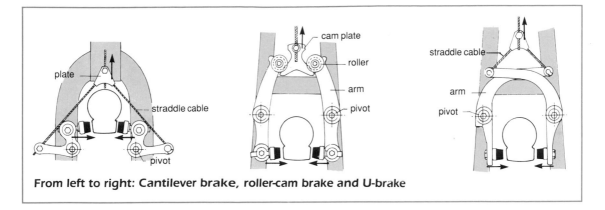

From left to right: Cantilever brake, roller-cam brake and U-brake

The Brakes

Today's mountain bikes once more have the same kinds of brakes installed on the first commercial models. These so-called cantilever brakes consist of lever arms mounted on bosses attached to the front fork blades and seat stays of the frame. There are still some other brake models around, and those often require different mounting positions for the pertinent bosses.

All mountain bike brakes are activated by means of easily reached brake levers on the handlebars via flexible bowden cables. At the brake, the control cable is connected to a straddle cable that hooks up to the two brake arms, pulling them together when the lever is applied. The angle of the connecting cable should be about 120—150 degrees to assure adequate braking force. The

Fisher Gemini tandem. Although the outback is not the place to try out your tandem riding skills for the first time (it is more difficult than you might think), mountain bike tandem designs have many virtues, since the heavy loads exerted on them, even when riding on paved roads, call for the same kind of reinforcements as used for mountain bikes.

cables should be flexible and as thick as possible consistent with the diameter of the outer cables. A teflon liner inside the outer cable helps reduce friction.

Accessories

"If you don't get anything else, at least buy a lock and use it every time you leave the bike unattended"

This is not the place to go into great detail, since they will be mentioned in Chapter 6. Just the same, I should mention what kind of useful accessories are available specifically for use with mountain bikes. If you don't get anything else, at least buy a lock and use it every time you leave the bike unattended.

As for the other options, there are luggage racks and fenders, or mudguards, toeclips for the pedals and water bottles, special lighting systems for night riding, gizmos to prevent the chain from getting caught and ones to adjust the seat height while riding. And, of course, there are all the goodies that are also available for regular bikes, often slightly modified for mountain bike use.

With this overview of the bike in hand, we can now, in the next chapters, get down to the brass tacks of handling the machine, starting off with the most important aspect — competent use of those many gears that are standard on the mountain bike.

CHAPTER 3

Using the Gears

"Gears by themselves won't make you get up those steep trails: You have to learn how to use them."

Typical front and rear derailleurs designed for mountain bike use. Gene Anthony photos.

THE 18 OR 21 GEARS with which the mountain bike is equipped by themselves won't make you just get up those steep trails. You have to learn to handle them correctly to get the most out of the bike. That is the subject of the present chapter. After introducing the components of the system, I'll explain just what gears will do for you, then you'll get to know the nuts and bolts of the gearing system's components, after which both the process of gear selection and the actual hands-on techniques for correct gear shifting will be covered.

To find out how to maintain and adjust the gears, you are referred to Chapter 12, which is devoted to maintenance. Reference tables for the selection of the gears are contained in the Appendix, wheraas their use will be explained in this chapter.

"Index shifters have a stepped ratchet mechanism inside that stops the cable in predetermined positions."

The Parts of the Gearing System

Mountain bike gearing systems comprise the components shown in the illustration. At the rear wheel a rear derailleur shifts the chain sideways to an appropriate sprocket, and the same is done in the front between the three chainrings by means of the front derailleur, or changer.

The derailleurs are operated by means of handlebar-mounted shifters: the one on the right controls the front derailleur, the one on the left the rear derailleur. Shifters and derailleurs are connected via flexible cables.

Index Derailleurs

The difference between the modern index derailleurs and old-fashioned friction models lies mainly in the shifters and the cables. Index shifters have a stepped ratchet mechanism inside that stops the cable in predetermined positions, coinciding with derailleur positions for particular sprockets. Most over-the-bar versions have a supplementary lever that allows shifting between the index mode and a friction mode, in which intermediate positions can be reached (to allow full use of the gears even when the index system is out of adjustment).

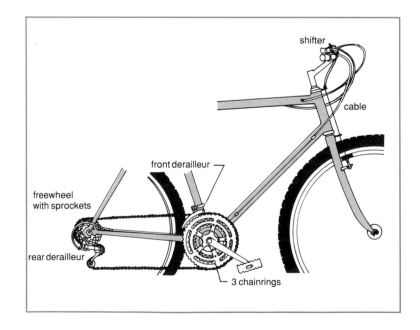

The parts of the gearing system.

The cables used for index gearing are thicker and stiffer than conventional cables to eliminate real or apparent stretch, which would throw the system out of adjustment. Their length is usually preset for a certain configuration, since they are very hard to cut. These cables also have alow-friction nylon or teflon liner and do not require lubrication.

Since 1990, most mountain bikes come with double-button levers mounted under the handlebars. These allow operation without moving the hands: push the top button to shift up, the bottom button to shift down. There are some differences between the available models, but most are so complicated that the manufacturers rightfully warn against taking them apart when they don't work properly: You'll have to replace the whole unit.

Shimano's version no longer has a friction mode to allow for maladjustment. As mentioned in Chapter 1, it is only available as a combined unit integrating brake lever and gear shifter. This is a particularly consumer-hostile approach. SunTour's version is mounted separately and also includes a small-step ratchet to allow non-index shifting, if necessary.

Fancy gear from Campagnolo. Above, regular index shifters and Bullet twist grip shifters. Below, mountain bike rear derailleur.

The Rear Derailleur

Essentially every rear derailleur consists of a hinged, spring-tensioned parallelogram mechanism with which a spring-tensioned cage, with its two chain guide wheels can be moved sideways, shifting the chain from one sprocket to another. The most significant differences in design are between older European models with a hanging parallelogram and a the Japanese and all modern ones with a more horizontal mechanism. Then there is the difference between models with long cages and short ones, between the mounting location for the cage, and between straight and slanted parallelogram mountings.

Essentially all mountain bikes have a rear derailleur of the so-called slant pantograph design, since these lend themselves better to the use of index shifting mechanisms. This design minimizes the distance between the chain and the sprocket teeth, making for more positive shifting. The models with a long cage, preferably pivoted at a point between the two chain guide wheels,

"The most important adjusting device for the modern derailleur is the cable tension adjuster."

Moving along in a 'two-foot gear,' Joey Peterson climbs a steep section during the NORBA Nationals near Santa Barbara.
Gordon Bainbridge photo.

are more easily adapted to large differences between sprocket sizes (i.e. very wide-range gearing).

Most models are marked to show the range of sprocket sizes and the amount of 'chain wrap' for which they are suitable. In some cases, the cage can be attached to the body in several different locations, each representing a certain range of sprocket sizes. The amount of chain wrap for which a derailleur is suitable indicates how big the difference between the combinations *largest chainring, largest sprocket* on the one hand, and *smallest chainring, smallest sprocket* on the other may be.

The most important adjusting device for the modern derailleur is the cable tension adjuster. In addition, the extreme limits of travel are adjusted with the set-stop, or limit, screws. In the case of the slant pantograph model, there is an additional adjusting screw with which the angle between the parallelogram and the horizontal plane can be adjusted to achieve the greatest degree of chain-wrap around the sprocket consistent with smooth shifting, following the description in the manufacturer's instruction leaflet.

Although most derailleurs are installed directly to a threaded lug on the RH rear drop-out nowadays, simple bikes may lack this feature. In that case, the derailleur is mounted on an adaptor plate that is held between the drop-out and the wheel axle nut or quick-release. Both adaptor plates and drop-outs are generally designed for specific derailleurs, which work best when certain distances are adhered to. This locks you into equipment from a specific manufacturer, so it is preferable not to experiment with a different make or model of derailleur than the one for which the drop-out on the frame was designed.

The Front Derailleur

The mountain bike's front derailleur simply consists of a hinge mechanism that moves an otherwise fixed cage sideways to guide the chain over one chainring or another. Mountain bike models have a pretty long cage to handle the big differences between chainring sizes. The adjustment mechanism is usually limited to a set of set-stop screws to adjust the range of lateral travel.

Most modern versions have a hinge mechanism that

does more than just move the cage sideways. In addition, they tend to lift the chain towards the larger one as they move to the right, drop down as they move to the left.

Instead of a regular front derailleur, there is one system on the market that does the same job in a more sophisticated manner. This is the Browning system, available from SunTour under the name BEAST. It is an electrically controlled system in which sections of the chainrings are hinged and move sideways to deliver the chain to the next chainring. Although one may object to battery-powered technology on the otherwise perfectly manually operated bike, there is no doubt something to be said for the ease with which this system shifts the chain even under the most difficult conditions (all other front derailleurs shift rather more reluctantly as long as the chain is under tension, as when cycling uphill).

Derailleur Controls

Both front and rear derailleurs are operated by means of shift levers via bowden cables. On a mountain bike, the shift levers are either mounted on top or below the handlebars, where they are readily accessible without taking the hand off the handlebars. Some hybrid bikes and competition models with drop handlebars use bar-end shifters instead, which are just as easy to operate — but only as long as you hold the bars at their ends, which is not really where most people hold dropped handlebars.

In addition to these regular models, there are twist grip-operated systems. Grip- Shift was the first one out and was mainly used on triathlon bikes with handlebar extensions. Meanwhile, Campagnolo and Sachs-Huret both introduced something similar for installation on the ends of regular mountain bike handlebars. Whatever design is used, the shifter for the rear derailleur is mounted on the right, the one for the front derailleur on the left.

Gearing Theory

The principle of the gearing system is the idea of adapting the transmission ratio between cranks and rear wheel to the difficulty of the terrain. Under favorable con-

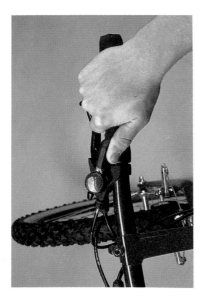

Shifting options. Above, currently popular under-the-bar shifter. Below, conventional over-the-bar thumb shifter.

"A high gear is achieved when a large chainring is combined with a small sprocket."

ditions — when the resistances are low, e.g. going downhill or on smooth surfaces with a favorable wind — the driven rear wheel can rotate quite a bit faster than the cranks, propelling the bike at a high speed without pedaling excessively fast. This is referred to as a high gear and is achieved when a large chainring is combined with a small sprocket. Under unfavorable conditions — when resistances are high, e.g. uphill or on soft ground —, a low gear is selected, achieved with a small chainring and a large sprocket, so the rear wheel does not turn much faster (in extreme cases even slower) than the cranks.

It will be instructive to compare the situation on a level road with that on an incline. The example will be based on a cyclist who can maintain an output of 100 W (i.e. about 0.13 hp). On a level road without head wind, this will suffice to progress at 30 km/h (about 20 mph). If the road goes up by 8%, the same output only allows a speed of 10 km/h (about 6.5 mph).

If the gearing ratio were fixed, the pedaling rate would have to be three times as high in the first case as it is in the second. Conversely, the forces applied to the pedals would be three times as high when pedaling slowly uphill as they would be pedaling fast on the level road. However, the muscles and joints work better if the pedal force is limited, even if this requires a higher pedaling speed. Thus, the uphill ride would be particularly tiring, even though the same total output is delivered — not because of the output, but because of the high forces at low muscle speeds.

This predicament is solved with the use of gearing. It allows selecting the ratio between pedaling and riding speed in such a way that the pedaling force remains within the limits of comfort by allowing an adequately high pedaling speed, regardless of the riding speed. Conversely, it is possible to keep the pedaling rate within the comfortable range when conditions are so easy that one would otherwise have to pedal extremely fast to deliver the available output.

To achieve this, the relatively untrained fitness cyclist might select a gear in which he maintains a pedaling rate of 70 rpm while each crank revolution brings him forward by about 7.15 m. This results in a speed of 70 x 7.15 x 60 = 30,030 m/h, or 30 km/h. On an incline, he may maintain the same pedaling rate and out-

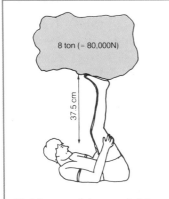

8 ton (= 80,000N)

37.5 cm

Raising an 8-ton weight over 37.5 cm is one way to bring an output of 300 watt. Gearing makes it easier, using lower forces at a higher leg speed.

> "It is unrealistic to assume that the same output level and pedaling speeds are always maintained."

put level, but might select a gear that brings him forward only 2.30 m per crank revolution, which results in a speed of 70 x 2.40 x 60 =10,080 m/h, or 10 km/h. Either way, pedaling speed and muscle force remain unchanged.

Actually, it is unrealistic to assume that the same output level and pedaling speeds are always maintained. All riders put in more effort when climbing than when riding on the level. The example shows what is possible, even though the actually selected gears and speeds may vary a little one way or the other. To adhere to the example would require a very wide range of gears, even for rather moderate terrain differences.

A typical configuration for a mountain bike might include a range of 13 to 26 teeth in the rear and 26, 36 and 46 teeth in the front, resulting in a top gear that is (46/13)/(26/26) = 3.54 times as high as the lowest gear.

Despite this formidable range, these gears are still not quite spread far enough apart to allow pedaling at the same rate and force level under all circumstances from steep uphills to easy cruising. But the human body is adaptable enough to make up for the difference.

Gear Designation

Although one could refer to the particular gear ratio by simply stating the size of chainring and sprocket, this is not a satisfactory method. It would not easily reveal that e.g. 46/26 gives the same gear ratio as 26/13, namely 2.0 in both cases. Obviously, it becomes completely impossible to compare bikes with different wheel sizes. To overcome these problems, two methods have been developed, referred to as *gear number* and *development*, respectively.

Gear number is a rather archaic method that remains inexplicably used to this day in the English speaking world. It references the equivalent wheel size of a directly driven wheel that would correspond to the same gear. To calculate the gear number, use the following formula:

$N \quad = \quad D_{wheel} \times T_{front} / T_{rear}$

where:

$N \quad = \quad$ gear number in inches

Gear designation methods: gear number in inches and development in meters.

"For mountain biking situations, typical high gears are in the vicinity of 80 inches, while the lowest gears are below 30 inches."

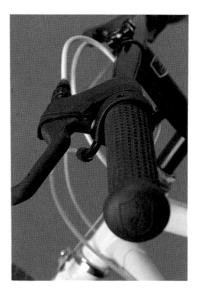

Shifting with the Campagnolo Bullet twist grip.
H. C. Smolik photo.

D_{wheel} = actual outside wheel diameter in inches
T_{front} = number of teeth, chainring
T_{rear} = number of teeth, sprocket.

For mountain biking situations, typical high gears are in the vicinity of 80 inches, while the lowest gears are below 30 inches.

The development designation, used in the rest of the world, is easier to visualize: it represents the distance traveled per crank revolution, measured in meters. To calculate it, use the following formula:

$$D = \pi \times D_{wheel} \times T_{front} / T_{rear}$$

where:

D = development in meters
π = 3.14
D_{wheel} = actual outside wheel diameter in m
T_{front} = number of teeth, chainring
T_{rear} = number of teeth, sprocket.

A typical high gear may be around 7—8 m, while a low gear may be 2.0—2.5 m.

Neither of these gear designations needs to be calculated once you know how they are determined. The tables in the Appendix provide a reference for their determination on the basis of the mountain bike's typical 26-inch wheels.

The Gear Progression

Ergonomically, it is best to select the gears in such a way that the difference between them is larger in the range of low gears than it is in high gears. This is achieved by selecting the sprocket sizes so that the smaller sprockets differ less from each other than the biggest sprockets. The best ratio is obtained when the percentage steps of the sprocket sizes remain approximately the same. Thus, the high gears are closer together than the low ones.

Take, as an example, a series of 7 sprockets from 13 to 25. At first, it may seem logical to assign them as follows: 13, 15, 17, 19, 21, 23 and 25. The difference is always 2 teeth. However, between 15 and 13 that amounts to 2/15 = 0.15, or 15%, while between 23 and 25 it is only 2/25 = 0.08, or 8%. This incongruity becomes even more dramatic as wider-range gearing is used.

In mountain biking, the choice of gears is divided into three clearly defined ranges as determined by the different chainrings in the front. Since mountain bikes are often ridden under conditions where shifting with the front chainring must be minimized, this makes perfect sense, because you just don't have the time to fidget around shifting back and forth. At the beginning of the uphill section, you go to the smallest chainring and do your shifting with the rear derailleur from there on. On the downhill and on level road you keep the chain on the big chainring in the front, and everywhere in between you use the intermediate chainring.

Especially when systems with seven sprockets are used, the extreme gears that cross over the chain from the smallest chainring in the front to the smallest sprocket in the back or vice versa from big to big should be avoided. The resulting lateral chain deflection causes both high wear and reduced efficiency of the drive train. It will be virtually impossible to adjust the derailleurs in such a way that the chain does not rub against the derailleur cage in the extreme gears.

"You just don't have the time to fidget around shifting back and forth."

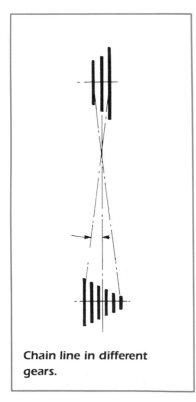

Chain line in different gears.

Gearing Practice

Sorry about all that theoretical stuff, but I feel a sound understanding of the theory helps doing things right in practice. Once you understand what you are supposed to do and why you are doing it, the following instructions will be all you need to follow to shift competently.

☐ Shift while pedaling forward with low pedaling force, meaning you may have to put in some extra effort just before the shift. This is especially important when shifting with the front derailleur.

☐ Front derailleur shifts between different chainrings are achieved with the RH shifter.

  a. If your bike is equipped with under-the-bar shifters, change onto the next bigger chainring (higher gear range) by pushing the top button in fully and letting it return. To shift to the next smaller chainring (lower gear range), push the lower button in fully and let it return. Repeat for each step.

  b. If the bike has over-the-bar thumb shifters,

"It takes practice. Even once you can do it motorically, you have to do it consciously and keep practicing."

change to the next bigger chainring (higher gear range) by pushing the shifter counterclockwise by one notch, or further to shift up another step; the next smaller chainring is reached by pushing the thumb shifter clockwise by one notch, or further to shift down another step.

☐ Rear derailleur shifts between different sprockets are achieved with the LH shifter.

a. If your bike is equipped with under-the-bar shifters, change onto the next smaller sprocket (higher gear) by pushing the top button in fully and letting it return. To shift to the next bigger sprocket (lower gear), push the lower button in fully and let it return. Repeat to shift another step.

b. If the bike has above-the-bar thumb shifters, change to the next smaller sprocket (higher gear) by pushing the shifter counterclockwise by one notch, or further to shift up another step. The next bigger sprocket (lower gear) is reached by pushing the thumb shifter clockwise by one notch, or further to shift down another step.

☐ It takes practice. First put the bike on a stand (or any other way with the rear wheel raised off the ground) and shift 'dry', observing just what happens as you shift and thinking about what effect it has. Next, simply take the bike on easy terrain and keep shifting up and down and down and up until you get a feel for the procedure. Finally venture out in more difficult terrain and try to do it there.

☐ Even once you can do it motorically, you have to do it consciously and keep practicing. Think ahead of time how you should shift and make a point of shifting frequently until it becomes automatic. Always think ahead about which chainring you should select for the next quarter of a mile, and which sprocket for the next couple of yards: the steeper you are going uphill or the harder the terrain, the lower the gear.

☐ When you are stopped, select a low gear to get going again, but make sure it is just high enough to work up enough speed to gather momentum fast enough to keep your balance.

CHAPTER 4

Basic Riding Skills

"There will be a couple of things to learn and practice if you want to ride off-road with any degree of confidence."

Brian Fairchild at the Great Flume in the Sierras. Gordon Bainbridge photo.

I'LL ASSUME you know how to ride a bike. Even so, there will be a couple of things to learn and practice if you want to ride off-road with any degree of confidence. This and the next chapter are devoted to the skills necessary to master that trick. First, in the present chapter, I shall cover the most general concepts of steering and balancing, accelerating and braking, uphill and downhill, on smooth surfaces, on rocky ones and on loose soil. Armed with the confidence that comes with having mastered and understood those skills, the next chapter will be devoted to the more complex tasks — all the way up to trick riding, if you are so inclined. Before getting down to the skills though, let's make sure you are sitting comfortably.

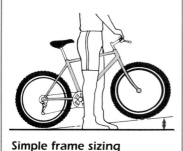

Simple frame sizing method

"Standing over the frame between the seat and the handlebars, you should be able to raise the front wheel off the ground by about 5 inches."

Sizing the Bike to the Rider

No single factor is more important to the comfort and confidence of the rider than the correct fit, and that's what this section is all about. It's a matter of having the right size bike, but even more of adjusting it optimally. It's easy enough once you know what you have to achieve.

First make sure the bike is approximately the right size. The best time to do that is of course when you buy it, but even if you already own a bike, you'd do well to check how well proportioned it is. If it's not, you may have to make some compromises along the way — and buy a better fitting bike the next time, if you get a chance. Standing over the frame between the seat and the handlebars, you should be able to raise the front wheel off the ground by about 5 inches. If you can't, the bike is probably too big for you, at least under very demanding conditions, where you will want to be able to reach the ground. You can ride just about any bike as long as the pedals stay within your reach, but it is safest and most comfortable on a bike of the right size.

Next, set the saddle at the right height, using either the seat quick-release or, if your bike does not have one, a wrench to undo and tighten the binder bolt in the back of the seat lug. In the basic, relaxed riding position, you should be able to reach the pedal with the heel of the foot when the pedal is in its lowest position with the knee straight but not straining. Only for difficult downhill stretches will you need to lower the seat relative to this position, so it makes sense to mark the seatpost somehow to allow you to quickly readjust it to this

Bike frame size as well as seat height depend on the rider's leg length. See the explanations in the text and the table in the Appendix for recommended sizes.

Inseam leg length, frame size and seat height

The relaxed position

Confident riding requires a
perfect fit, the mastery of
basic riding skills — and lots
of conscious practice.
Photo courtesy Gary Fisher
MountainBikes.

height. If your bike has a Hite-Rite seat adjusting fitting
(a coil spring connecting the seat tube with the seat lug),
make sure it is set so that it automatically returns to
this position when released. Note that the heels-on-
pedal mode only applies to adjusting the saddle height,
not to riding: when you ride the bike, the ball of the foot
should be over the pedal axle.

In some cases, the forward position of the seat may
also need adjusting. The optimum position is considered
the one whereby the knee joint (recognized as the little
bump on the side of the knee just behind the knee cap)
is perpendicular above the center of the pedal axle when
the crank points forward horizontally. Although I find
this position generally the most acceptable for my own
use, there is no scientific evidence of its superiority, so
feel free to go further forward or back if you are not comfortable in the long run. You may want to refer to Chapter 12 for a description of the angular and forward adjustment of the saddle.

Once the saddle is in the right position, the next step
is to adjust the handlebars. In the relaxed position, they
should be about 2—3 inches lower than the seat. If you
put it higher, you will not only look like a klutz on the
bike, you will likely ride like one too, since it puts too
much of your weight on the saddle, unnecessarily loading your buttocks and spinal column and making it harder to control the bike.

The horizontal distance between the seat and the
handlebars can only be correctly judged once these first
adjustments have been carried out. And it's not something you can measure — you have to *feel* comfortable.
Most modern mountain bikes stretch the rider out too
far, the (usually fallacious) argument being that off-road
racers sit that way. Perhaps they do, but then it is not
for optimum comfort but in order to get up off the saddle
and apply the weight directly over the pedals when
climbing standing up. That's probably not what you
have in mind, so that's not how the bike should be set
up. Although the distance can be decreased by moving
the seat further forward, it is generally better to leave
that adjustment alone and replace the handlebar stem
instead.

When adjusting the height of the saddle or the handlebars, make sure the seatpost and the stem are held
into the frame by at least 65 mm (2.5 inches) to assure a

The relationship between body and bike lean and steering is critical for balancing the bike. To turn to the right, bike and body must be leaning in the same direction, otherwise the bike will fall over. The sharper the curve, and the higher the speed, the more distinct should be the lean.

"Even to ride a straight line, you have to perform quite a complex steering and balancing act."

firm hold. Many stems and seatposts are engraved with a maximum projection mark; if yours are not, you can take them out, measure the right distance and make a mark with an indelible marking pen yourself.

Finally the width of the handlebars is not sacred. Many bikes are still supplied with excessively wide bars, and it may make good sense to cut a piece off each end with a hacksaw, filing the burr off afterwards. If you have difficulty removing the handgrips, lift them with a screwdriver and squirt some dishwashing liquid in. Remove that stuff before reinstalling them, though — in fact, it may be necessary to apply some hairsetting spray to the inside before installing them to make sure they stay put.

Steering and Balancing

Your mountain bike is not steered the same way as your car. Even to ride a straight line, you have to do perform a quite complex steering and balancing act, which fortunately you learned subconsciously when you first learned to ride a bike (this is quite tricky for newcomers though, and is the reason why it is so hard for adults to learn to ride).

Simply going straight on the bike is in reality more like following a long stretched serpentine, deviating now to the left, now to the right, each time using a steering maneuver to get back in line. In fact, once you deviate to the left, you don't get back to the original track by steering to the right, because that would bring you crashing down, as your center of gravity would be too far to the left while the bike is moving away from you to the right. Instead, you steer just a little further to the left, inducing an imbalance the other way, with you leaning to the right, setting you up just right to steer back to the right.

Although you can probably do it right without thinking about it (and it may prove harder to do when you do think about it), I suggest you go out to an area without traffic and try to do it consciously, so you begin to get a feel for what you are doing. This will be useful in off-road cycling, where you get into much more difficult situations and where only a thorough understanding of balancing gives you the ability to avoid a fall.

Once you have developed a feel for what happens

when riding an almost straight line, balancing your way forward as straight as you can, it is time to do the same with turns. There are two kinds of turns, which I call the *natural* and the *forced* method respectively.

The natural curve is ridden when you have plenty of time and room. You simply wait until the bike is leaning the right way and, rather than oversteering to regain balance, you leave the handlebars alone until the lean is so pronounced that it corresponds to the turn. That's when you steer in the appropriate direction to make a gradual, large-radius turn.

When there is less time and room for the maneuver, the forced steering technique is used, and this too calls for a few practice sessions. To make a sharp turn, first induce a lean in the appropriate direction (i.e. to the right if you want to turn right); then, as the lean becomes quite pronounced, catch yourself by steering in the direction of the lean. To regain your balance after the turn, let the bike oversteer until you begin to lean in the opposite direction and then steer back against the

Frame geometry is what makes a mountain bike and determines its steering and handling characteristics. This backyard special by Rich Borthwick at Big Mountain, California, handles just as well as any commercial mountain bike.
Gordon Bainbridge photo.

Comparison of natural (left) and forced turn (right)

direction of the lean, bringing you on track again.

Don't just read this: *do it*, and don't take my word for it, experience it. Defy the theory and see what happens when you just turn the handlebars when you are not leaning in the appropriate direction, or try to lean without steering. It's only by practicing these simple basic steering and balancing techniques in a quiet area, that you will master the bike enough to ride it confidently.

Braking

As often as not, the mountain bike's brakes are not so much used to make it stop on a dime but rather to slow down to a more manageable speed. Instead, the brakes

As you brake, your mass center is transferred forward. For a quick stop, you have to move far back and keep your mass center as low as possible, so you keep control over the bike.

As shown on the left, the rear wheel starts to lift when the front brake is applied, especially on the downhill.

On a steep downhill, a sudden application of the front brake can cause the cyclist to topple over the handlebars. And not every rider has the skills demonstrated here by Matt Bottomley to get out of it safely.
Gene Anthony photos.

are more typically used gradually, either to keep the bike under control or to get down to such a speed that particular maneuvers can safely be carried out. Even so, occasionally, you have to brake really hard and get the maximum stopping power out of them.

There is quite a difference between what is possible in terms of braking between the various situations. On level ground it is a lot easier than on a downhill, or even an uphill, where slowing down is of course rarely a problem but keeping just enough speed to keep balancing is. Then there is a difference between braking on solid ground or on dirt, on rocks, ice, gravel, in rain, snow or mud.

"First get a feel for what is achieved by braking on hard level ground."

First get a feel for what is achieved by braking on hard level ground. Go out and practice, taking mental notes of the way the bike reacts when applying just the front brake, just the rear, or both simultaneously. There is a theory behind the whole braking phenomenon, and you can read about it in some of my more technical books (e.g. *Bicycle Technology*, also published by Bicycle Books). Here I will not strain your patience with too much technical detail, so I'll just summarize the conclusions:

☐ On level ground, the effect of the front brake is about twice that of the rear brake, and the maximum braking possible with the rear brake is limited by loss of traction of the rear tire as the weight distribution is shifted forward during braking.

☐ On the descent, the same forward shift of the rider's weight limits the maximum braking possible with the front brake, so there it becomes important to divide braking between the front and the rear brake, and to avoid building up speed to the point where hard braking becomes necessary.

☐ When the rims are wet, the friction of the brake blocks is drastically reduced, resulting in much deteriorated braking, meaning you'd better keep the speed down even more and start braking very early.

☐ When you brake in a curve, the bike tends to skid out sideways towards the outside. Although it makes for interesting photographs of mountain bike action, it does not necessarily please everybody, and generally only reduces control over the bike. The more ac-

Flying start: To get on the bike while running, swing one leg over the saddle and try to catch the pedals. Gene Anthony photo.

ceptable way to keep your speed within control is to apply the brakes on the straight run to get down to a manageable speed *before* you reach the curve, and let go while actually riding the curve.

As with so many other techniques, braking should be consciously practiced, starting on level ground and working towards more difficult terrain. Do it. It will pay off when the situation in the terrain becomes critical.

Once you have come to a standstill, if that's what you brake down to, there is usually no need to actually get off the bike. Just lean the bike over in one direction to get one leg on the ground if you can find something high enough; if not, move forward off the saddle and straddle the top tube, from where it is easy enough to get back on the seat by pedaling half a stroke once you want to get going again.

"As with so many other techniques, braking should be consciously practiced."

Starting and Accelerating

You can't always be going at the same speed, sometimes you have to increase it, even if only to get going at all. When accelerating, whether it is to increase your speed or to get going at all from a stop, traction sometimes becomes a problem, especially on steep inclines and loose gravel. You need all the weight on the rear wheel you can get to maximize traction, yet you need enough on the front wheel to keep the steering under control.

Get going gradually, without any sudden spurts of power, which tend to lead to skidding. Don't start off in your very lowest gear, even when it is quite steep, because you would not get enough momentum. Stand up and balance your weight, shifting it between the front and the rear enough to keep the front wheel on the ground and the rear wheel from skidding. It is another one of those things that require practice, which is most easily gained doing it consciously, paying attention only to that particular aspect of bike handling.

Sarah Ellis demonstrating how to accelerate while going uphill.
Gene Anthony photo.

Climbing

Climbing requires disproportionally more energy than riding on level ground at the same speed. That's what gears were invented for: they make it possible to sacrifice some speed in exchange for momentum, while

Taking a curve on the downhill without skidding or slowing down requires concentration.

allowing you to pedal at the same comfortable rate. Heed the advice given in Chapter 3 with respect to the use of derailleur gearing.

In some ways, particularly on loose dirt, climbing is very akin to accelerating. Balance is everything. Although many mountain bikes are designed to go uphill well without a need to get off the saddle, many of the more aggressively designed frame geometries so popular these days are not. Here you simply have to get up and consciously divide your weight between the front and the rear of the bike. Practice this too.

Descending

The first mountain bikes were pure downhill machines. Their long wheelbase and low rider position made them easy to control on a descent. Today's mountain bikes are shorter and steeper and must be ridden downhill with more care. If it is quite steep, sit far back on the saddle, or go as far as staying behind the saddle, stretching forward and keeping your weight as low as possible to keep your balance. Control your speed carefully with the brakes, following the advice given above for braking.

These simple techniques are really only the beginning, and in Chapter 5 you will learn quite a few more tricks that are much more sophisticated. At first, even if you have considerable experience riding a bike under normal conditions, it will pay off to practice each of these techniques very consciously, so you thoroughly master them. That will help you enjoy the use of your mountain bike to the fullest.

Advanced Off-Road Techniques

"It really gets a magical quality once you truly master the art of controlling the bike."

ALTHOUGH IT IS POSSIBLE to ride and enjoy the mountain bike with the basic skills described in the preceding chapter, it really gets a magical quality once you truly master the art of controlling the bike. In this chapter, you'll learn how to make the bike do just what you want it to under all circumstances. It's a matter of becoming one with the bike.

Rough-Surface Riding

On the road, most people just sit on their bikes, leaning on the seat with most of their weight. If you try to do

Taking the plunge at the Spring Runoff Race at Sly Park, California.
Gordon Bainbridge photo.

Also learn to handle the bike by carrying it when needed, holding the frame and handlebars as shown here. Gene Anthony photo.

that on rough surfaces, you'll lose control of the bike pretty fast. The main mass on a bicycle is that of its rider, and putting some suspension between it and the road helps a lot. Do that in three steps:

☐ Distribute the weight over seat, handlebars and pedals more equitably.

☐ Use your arms and legs as shock absorbers.

☐ Shift your weight between front and back, high and low in response — better yet in anticipation — of shocks from surface unevennesses.

Unlike the early mountain bikes, which were purely designed to sit, whether going uphill or down, its modern counterpart is short and steep enough to comfortably stretch up to unload from the seat and load the pedals more, or to move forward and up to load the handlebars.

Find a really rough stretch of road or trail and compare the effect of riding over it at different speeds both ways — remaining seated and getting up, using your arms and legs to absorb the shock. You will not only be more comfortable doing the latter, you will also retain full control over the bike and you'll be able to ride much faster.

Balancing the Bike

Basic to the whole idea of growing together with the bike is your feeling of balance. Try standing still while sitting on the bike without falling over to the left or the right. Not easy, what? To do it, you have to understand what keeps the bike from falling over: the same relationship between lean, steering angle and center of gravity that was discussed in Chapter 4 for riding straight lines and curves. Standing still can be seen as the ultimate straight line. Rather than riding a horizontal serpentine, you perform the same act on the spot.

Start off by just slowing down: ride a very slow straight line. Notice how the extent over which you have to steer one way or the other to keep your balance become bigger? The trick is trying to keep those deviations to a minimum. The lower your forward speed the more critical for your balance even a slight degree of lean becomes. To regain balance after even a modest lean, you need to angle the steering more sharply. So your steer-

"The lower your forward speed, the more critical for your balance even a slight degree of lean becomes."

"Always remain conscious of how you are leaning and steering, until you have an almost instinctive feel for the complex relationships involved."

Practice balancing and controlling the bike. Establish at which point the front wheel and when the rear wheel starts lifting off when braking. But try to keep the bike under control while you do so. Gene Anthony photos.

ing angle is an indicator for your balance: if you don't need to steer very sharply at any given low speed, that shows you are better balanced.

Find a safe, level spot to practice, and keep working on going straight and riding curves at increasingly slower speeds, until you are indeed almost standing still. As you do so, always remain conscious of how you are leaning and steering, until you have an almost instinctive feel for the complex relationships involved in the act of balancing the bike at minimal speed.

Once you get down to speeds so low that you are obviously not going anywhere, and feel comfortable doing it. get ready for the next step. Find yourself a very slight slope. Actually, roads are often better for this next stage of practice, because the very camber of most roads, i.e. the way the slightly higher center of the road slopes down to the slightly lower sides for drainage, is just about right for the purpose. The smoothness of the asphalt also helps by not contributing any imponderables.

Get out of the saddle and divide your weight over the two pedals, keeping the cranks horizontal. Point the front wheel towards the higher ground and try to stand still. Yes, you'll start to roll back if you don't keep the force on the pedals — but don't apply the brakes until you start rolling forward. Respond to any tendency to fall over one way or the other by turning the handlebars ever so slightly to point the front wheel in the same direc-

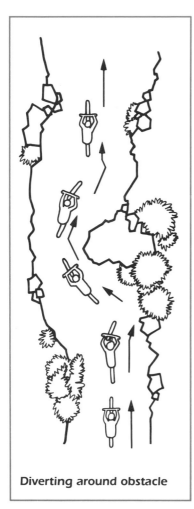

Diverting around obstacle

Below: Your first step in getting off the ground.

tion, without rolling either forward or backward.

It's a skill that cannot be mastered overnight, and I'm not suggesting you keep working on it until you can do it — you'd get pretty frustrated. Practice for fifteen minutes and go on to more immediately gratifying things, riding your bike where you like, just be conscious of the whole steering and balancing act while doing so. Another practice session after the ride or later the same day is all you should devote to it for now. Repeat this each day for a week, and you'll find yourself remarkably well in control of the bike: You've learned to balance a stationary bike, and that's the first step in the mastery of the beast.

Getting Airborne

If you've ever had a BMX bike and did freestyle stuff at all, you may remember how to make one of those tiny machines take off. Well, it can be done on a mountain bike too, but it's a lot harder because it's designed to be ridden and you have to make compromises somewhere along the way. Here you will learn how to do it right.

The tool to use is the springiness of the tires. The basic requirement is a tire pressure that's just high enough to protect the tube yet low enough for your weight when it comes hard down on the rear wheel to go down by about ¾—1 inch. The energy released when this much air is compressed is enough to lift bike and rider up several feet.

Start practicing on a hard level surface (it won't work at all on soft ground because the energy, rather than being stored by the compressed air in the tire, goes into

Getting air is pretty exhilarating. Study the photo to see how an expert holds the bike: don't just sit in the saddle, but stretch up enough to absorb the shock when landing. And aim to land on the rear wheel first. Gene Anthony photo.

deforming the soil, which isn't going to spring back). Balance the bike standing still with the cranks horizontally — you just learned how to do that, so I hope you've been practicing. Pounce down with all your weight towards the rear of the bike to compress the rear tire in a short, snappy movement, and then just as snappily transfer your weight back forward. If all is well, the rear wheel comes off the ground.

The first few times you do this, it may seem like a pretty unspectacular performance. Keep doing it, interrupted by some riding to release the tension that is built up in your nerves more than in the tires. A couple of fifteen minute practice sessions two or three days in a row should pay off with quite spectacular results: you have mastered one third of the trick and it is time to get on with the next third, raising the front wheel off the ground.

To raise the front wheel is normally referred to as doing a wheely. And it is just as normal to do that by merely shifting your weight back quickly to unload the front wheel and briefly bring your mass center behind

Wheelies are not really the most important aspect of mountain biking. But they are a fine way to practice handling skills and confidence. Gene Anthony photo.

the rear wheel on account of the momentum of the body moving back. That's worth practicing, because it will be used in other stunts too. From a low speed or even standing still, balancing the bike now that you can do that, first keep your weight low and forward. Then throw it back with a decisive jolt, loading the rear wheel and releasing the front while pulling the handlebars up with you. Again, it may take some practice to perfect it, but this particular one is quite easy to learn.

To get both wheels off the ground, you want to do things a little more sophisticated than this, though. Since you have to combine it with the raising of the rear wheel eventually, the thing to do is to put an explosive charge under the front wheel, again in the form of tire compression, just as was done to get the rear wheel coming up. So don't just throw your weight back, but first pounce on the front end of the bike: quickly push down with your body weight on the handlebars, then immediately release it and throw your weight back as in a conventional wheely.

Finally, it will be time to combine the two movements of lifting the front and the rear wheel. Your first step will be to achieve it consecutively, first the front and then the rear. Balancing while standing still, push down hard on the front end and immediately release it, transferring the weight to the rear, compressing the rear tire quickly; then immediately release it by shifting your weight forward again. That's a horribly long sentence, but it should indeed beonea continuous movement that can not be broken up into steps. Do it as though you're reading and following the sentence as fast as possible. Practice, practice.

These are the steps to follow to cross an obstacle such as a boulder or a fallen tree trunk across your path.

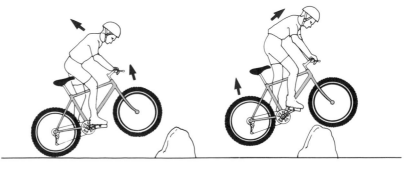

One way of climbing is in a relatively high gear, standing on the pedals and swaying from side to side, known as honking. Works best if there is good traction, i.e. not on loose gravel.

Suddenly, after a few days with two or three short practice session each, you can do it, and you'll wonder why it ever seemed so difficult. Notice how you graduated from putting one wheel up after the other to getting both of them up at the same time, without my telling you how it's done? It's nothing but the logical extension of what you were doing, and as you got better at it, those wheels started spending more time up in the air together simultaneously.

There are people — and I am not one of them myself — who can get both wheels to lift off at the same time. That's done by distributing the body weight over the front and the rear of the bike while pouncing down and at the same time compressing the body like a spring. When you raise the body just as suddenly by straightening your legs, arms and back, the whole unit of bike and rider starts to defy gravity and comes straight up. So they say, but if you are at all hesitant, you'll want to make sure nobody is watching as you clown around frustrated without getting any air. On the other hand, if you are more agile, coordinated and determined than I am, you will probably master this trick pretty soon too.

Taking Obstacles in Your Stride

The hopping routine described in the preceding section is as much a lesson in general bike handling as a practical device in itself. In the fine art of observed trials competition, it is an absolute prerequisite, but in everyday use you'll benefit more from the sense of bike control and balance derived from it than from the actual skill itself. In the real world things happen when you're moving

"The same techniques that are so useful in the boondocks also can be put to use under more prosaic circumstances."

Trials rider Kevin Norton showing a fine way to improve your skills. Special trials bikes are helpfull but not essential.
Gordon Bainbridge photo.

forward, not when you're standing still.

In your reality there will be the occasional (or sometimes frequent) obstacle in your path, ranging from ditches across the trail to potholes in city streets, from boulders and fallen trees to curbstones and railway tracks. It's consoling to know that the same techniques that are so useful in the boondocks also can be put to good use in the more prosaic circumstances of urban riding, as well as out on the trail.

The first step is to learn to go up a step, even if only to practice for bigger and better things. Find an area with a step in it of that is between six inches and one foot high and learn to approach it, lift the front wheel just before you get there, then hop onto it with the rear wheel, and keep riding. Perhaps you even want to practice it on an imaginary ridge: a chalkline drawn on an empty parking lot.

Next, try to do the same thing but now approach the ridge riding parallel to it and then hopping onto it sideways. That's actually the more typical situation in

When it is too steep to climb straight up, take a zig-zag course.
Gene Anthony photo.

"Shift your weight as you go through, so you don't get bogged down at the bottom of the pit."

real life, where many obstacles are almost parallel to your path rather than straight across. This is done by first briefly steering away from the ridge, and then immediately and snappily correcting the lean by steering back, so you shoot across the ridge with the front wheel almost perpendicular to it very briefly, before continuing in your original direction.

Whether jumping up a perpendicular or parallel ridge, once the front wheel is over, you have to unload the back by shifting your weight back to the front end of the bike and lift the rear wheel. You'll be surprised how easily it follows.

Your next step towards obstacle-running mastery will be jumping across things like tree trunks. Start off with something a little smaller, like a broomstick. You'll really notice it if you don't clear it with either wheel, but it is less intimidating and easier to place just where and how you want it. Front wheel up, rear wheel up and go. Practiced during a few fifteen-minute sessions, and quite soon, you will feel like graduating to treetrunks, boulders and the likes. As soon as you can do it, start applying each skill in your everyday riding so you reach perfect mastery gradually while enjoying what you do, rather than as a conscious exercise.

Overcoming Depressions

No, not the kind of depressions with which only a psychiatrist can help you: I mean holes in the ground rather than in your mind. Depressions can be seen as inverted obstacles. Only very wide ones can be ridden through, while smaller ones must be handled by trying to overfly them.

To ride through a wide depression, select your path so that it is as gradual as possible, often going through it under an angle. Shift your weight as you go through, so you don't get bogged down at the bottom of the pit. Just before you reach the lowest point, transfer your weight back so the front wheel gets unloaded. This way you gain badly needed traction on the way up and protect your bike as well as yourself (you might go over the handlebars if the bike suddenly comes to a stop as it bogs down). Transfer the weight back towards the front again as you climb out.

Bike handling is more than just riding it, especially in competition.
Photos by Gordon Bainbridge (left) and Andreas Schlüter (right).

"Once you get this far, you'll find you spend much less time in the saddle than you ever thought you would want to."

Now to clear a narrow trench or hole in the ground you have to do very much the same as to clear an obstacle projecting from the ground. The reason is that, unless you lift the wheels to make the bike go up at least a little, they'll just fall into the hole. So gain some speed and then, just before you get there, lift the front wheel as you've learned to do in the last section. As soon as the front wheel has come off the ground, transfer the weight back to get the rear wheel off the ground and start heading for safe ground with the front wheel, keeping the weight forward until also the rear wheel has cleared the depression.

Practice this exercise too as you go on your regular rides and you'll be surprised how much easier it is to ride in the roughest terrain. In effect, once you get this far, you'll find you spend much less time in the saddle than you ever thought you would want to. And even if you are in the saddle, you are always alert and always have your weight so well distributed over pedals, handlebars and seat, with your limbs slightly bent but tense enough to act as shock absorbers at all times. This way, obstacles become easy to overcome. It'll just be a matter of raising one part of your body relative to the other in a natural flow of movement. You've tamed the beast.

CHAPTER 6

Equipment and Accessories

"You need a minimum of two items for protection: a helmet for your head and a lock for the bike."

IN ADDITION to your mountain bike itself, there is a whole lot of other gear out there at the bike shop waiting for your credit card. Not all of it is equally useful and some different versions of things designed to do the same job exist. In this chapter, I shall introduce the most useful items and give you selection criteria, considering both items for you to wear and accessories to install on the bike.

Protection

You need a minimum of two items for protection: a helmet for your head and a lock for the bike. Although the subject of head protection and the injuries it prevents will be described more fully in the next chapter, I can tell you right here that you need one. Although there is not much car traffic in the outback, off-road cycling is ac-

Even if you don't buy any other gear, at least get a helmet and tie it down properly.
Gene Anthony photo.

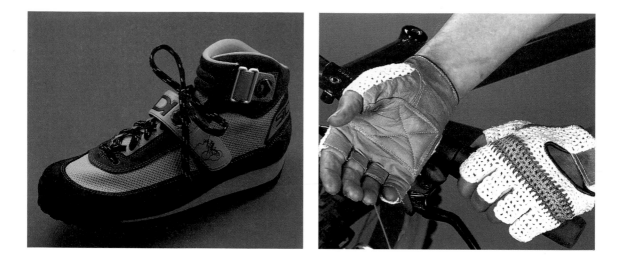

Special mountain biking shoes suitable for riding and walking and cycling gloves. Photos H.C. Smolik and Gene Anthony.

"The lock may not save lives, but it is more frequently called into action."

tually more dangerous than riding on the road, because it is falling off the bike on your head that causes most serious and fatal injuries.

All bicycle helmets sold at bike shops in the US provide adequate protection, because they meet the requirements of the ANSI helmet standard. Helmets with a fabric cover are popular, because they are light and look pretty much like normal headwear. Currently, there is a trend towards helmets with a smooth, hard, thin plastic outside layer. These slide over the ground better and may well help prevent neck injury when your fall takes place at speed.

Although I agree one should wear a helmet, I don't always do it myself! When climbing up a steep hill in hot weather, I find it just too uncomfortable for someone who perspires as much as I do. So that's where I take it off, and I feel the low speeds reached under such circumstances probably justify it. On the downhill, though, it belongs on your head, and the most useful gadget I can think of that someone ought to develop is a helmet clip to hold the thing on the bike and from which it could be easily grabbed. Anybody listening, out there?

The lock may not save lives, but it is more frequently called into action. Bike theft is so common, even in the outback, that you just can't go anywhere without it. Having had at least a dozen of the family's bikes stolen (I admit to having more bikes around waiting for the discriminating thief than most families), and having been offered even more obviously stolen bikes for sale, I can't

Mountain bike toeclips come in only one size: too big for anybody without flippers. Gene Anthony photo.

stress it enough: Buy a big U-lock, always carry it with you and always use it when you leave the bike, removing the front wheel and locking it up with the rest of the bike. Lock it all up to something immobile that is so big that the lock can't be lifted over the top.

Mountain Bike Clothing

It's OK to ride your bike in whatever is comfortable, but when you've tried out everything, you'll probably agree nothing is more comfortable than specific mountain bike clothing. Essentially, it's cycling dress adapted to the somewhat harsher demands of riding where you may fall. Even if you prefer to wear 'civies,' i.e. clothing that is not specifically designed with cycling in mind, there are a number of points to watch out for that will be covered in this section.

The points to keep in mind when selecting mountain bike clothing all have something to do with the specific kind of work cycling is. The clothing should meet the following criteria:

☐ It must be flexible to allow freedom of movement.

☐ It must fit tightly without pinching.

☐ It must absorb and wick away perspiration, giving off moisture to keep you cool when you perspire and insulate you when it is cold.

☐ It must be free from bulky seems or unnatural cuts interfering with movement.

☐ As much as possible, it should protect the body in places that may hit the road in case of a fall.

Regular bicycle clothing is suitable for most off-road cycling. However, you should look for particularly tough versions of these garments.

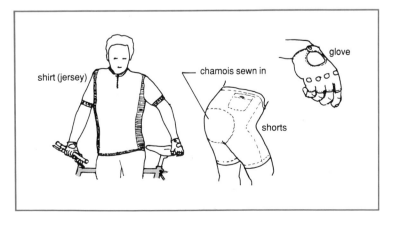

Top: Today's cycling wear — whether intended for road riding or mountain biking — is colorful and comfortable to wear.
Below: Warm, windproof jackets and colorful shorts. Photos Gene Anthony (top) and Cannondale (bottom).

Amongst the many fabrics used for bike clothing, there is one that does all those jobs better than any other. It is called wool and I am pleased to be able to report a resurgence of this natural miracle fabric. The only problem with wool is that it has to be treated very carefully: Wash it too hot and it will shrink; put it in the spin drier or hang it on a line and it will stretch out of shape; let it get wet on your body and it becomes heavy with water, taking forever and a day to dry and dragging you down like a ton of bricks.

The greatest advantage of some of the modern synthetic fibers is that they are best at what wool does worst — keep its shape. That property can be used to advantage by blending one or the other synthetic fiber in with the wool, providing the resilience that's needed without sacrificing wool's natural advantages. So, rather than falling for the admittedly more colorful and often cheaper fully synthetic garments, select those made of some blend with a fair percentage of wool — at least 50%.

The next question is what these things should look like. If you are going to ride in rough terrain, it is best to wear things with long sleeves and long legs, unless it is so hot that you just can't bear it. The extra length provides protection of sensitive places like the knees and the elbows. Besides, once these parts are covered, it is also possible to either integrate or add knee or elbow pads. Although you may not plan to fall off the bike, it is great to have this kind of protection: Not only does it help if you do fall, it also gives you the feeling of greater security, allowing you to ride much closer to your natural potential without fear. I've noticed the same with helmet wearing: when I don't wear the thing, I feel so insecure that I become a much less competent rider out of fear something may happen.

Gloves are quite useful in off-road cycling. They have a protective function too, because when you fall, you'll tend to stick out your hand to try and break the fall, and a pair of gloves may make the difference between walking home with bleeding hands and being able to ride the bike as if nothing happened. Conventional cycling gloves are padded and fingerless. They are fine to protect the hands in most cases, but for the really rough stuff you may want to wear gloves with fingers, even if it is not the kind of weather that normally calls for gloves.

"Look for a profile that is ribbed in such a way that the foot can still slide over the pedal."

Hite-Rite saddle height adjusting spring. Gene Anthony photo.

Cycling shoes distribute the pedaling force over as large an area as possible. Therefore they should have stiff soles. Normal cycling shoes have stiff soles that are completely smooth except for a metal clip (or some patent design to hold the shoe to the pedal). The disadvantage of these is that you can't possibly walk in them, and that makes them unsuitable for off-road use, where getting off the bike is on the order of the day. There are special mountain biking shoes with profile soles that are thicker yet quite firm, but just flexible enough to allow walking. Look for a profile that is ribbed in such a way that the foot can still slide over the pedal, otherwise you'll find it pretty hard to get your feet in or out of place, especially when using toeclips.

This is about all there is to say about special mountain biking wear. But keep in mind that the comfort gained by wearing the right outer garments should not be lost again on account of uncomfortable underwear. Undershorts, undershirts and socks are at least as important for your overall comfort as the items discussed above. Make sure they are flexible and comfortable, allowing freedom of movement, absorbing or transferring perspiration and without bulky seams (sometimes wearing things like socks inside out helps to keep the seams away from you). Special clothing for inclement weather will be covered in Chapter 9.

Mountain Bike Accessories

In addition to the lock mentioned at the beginning of this chapter, many accessories are available for use with the mountain bike. The most important ones will be covered below:

☐ tire pump
☐ water bottle
☐ luggage rack (carrier)
☐ lighting equipment
☐ fenders (mudguards)
☐ bicycle computer
☐ tool kit
☐ Hite-Rite
☐ 'odds and ends'

"Only if you carry a pump, can you get the full advantage of the mountain bike's fat tires"

Tire pump

Since the mountain bike's tires take a lot more air at a lower pressure, suitable pumps have a large stroke volume, at the expense of pressure. For at home, it is wise to also buy a stand pump, because it works so much faster and has a built-in pressure gauge. Only if you carry a pump, can you get the full advantage of the mountain bike's fat tires, which have to operate at different pressures depending on the terrain. Make a habit of actually adapting the tire pressure to the conditions, as explained in Chapter 2.

The lazy person's solution is the CO_2 cartridge. Convenient, small and light, but expensive to operate and a hassle to keep charged with cartridges, these things are less practical than they may at first appear to be: The gas contained in one of these is inadequate for fully inflating a chubby tire once you've had a puncture.

Water bottle

Most mountain bikes come equipped with bosses for the installation of one or more water bottles. Make sure you get a sturdy bottle cage (rather than an aluminum one) and choose the biggest water bottle. The most convenient location is on the downtube, but additional locations that may be available are below the downtube (hard to get at) and along the seat tube (tends to interfere with the installation of a lock or a pump).

Luggage racks

Special mountain bike luggage racks are made to fit the almost universally used mounting bosses on front fork and seat stays and the eyelets that should be present on all front and rear drop-outs except on out-and-out competition bikes. Strongest for their (low) weight are the tubular steel models, such as those made by California frame builder Bruce Gordon. Amongst the welded aluminum racks, those made by Blackburn probably have the best reputation for quality, even though there are many cheaper imitations that look identical.

An interesting aspect of luggage racks is their theft deterrent effect: It seems that those who steal bicycles for a living tend to judge a bike by its appearance and don't value one equipped with racks very highly (the use of fenders seems to have the same effect, although I still

Useful gadgets. A brace to rigidify the U-brake, a frame bag that doubles as a shoulder protector when carrying the bike, and a big water bottle. Barely visible: toeclips.
Villinger photo.

This is all you need by way of
tools for most longer rides.
Match the sizes of the tools
with the nuts and bolts used
on your bike.
Gene Anthony photo.

suggest you use a lock, even if your bike is loaded up
with accessories).

Lighting equipment

To ride off-road at night, you really need lots of light.
There are lead-acid battery operated units on the market
that feed 40 watt bulbs. These things only last for a
short time, so you may want to install a secondary light
of the same voltage but lower wattage to conserve juice
when it's not absolutely needed. It's perfectly wonderful
to ride with a full moon, but even then you should install at least a light in the front and a reflector or a red
light in the back.

Those who use their bikes for everyday transportation on the road should also install lights, but for their
use relatively modest lights run off e.g. two C-cells are
adequate. Use only lights with halogen (krypton) bulbs,
because they are brighter for the same electric consump-
tion and don't tend to blacken with age, as regular bulbs
do. On public roads, with mainly motor traffic, a reflector offers as much protection against danger from behind as a rear light.

Fenders

Using fenders to keep mud and water off your bike and
body is not considered cool in most parts of the US. I
must admit that, for one born and raised in some of the
wettest spots on earth, I also enjoy riding my bikes without those forever rattling and vibrating things. Besides,
in muddy terrain they cause more problems than they
solve, because the mud gets built up inside the fenders
until the wheel stops going around. Plastic clip-ons may
be an acceptable solution.

For road use in wet weather, permanently installed
fenders are a good idea, especially if you attach a mud
flap at the bottom of the one in the front (in fact, the
mud flap is so much more effective than the fender that
I consider a front fender primarily as a 'mudflap mount.'

Bicycle computer

Get one of those digital speed and distance recording
devices if you must, but they are of very limited sig-
nificance in off-road cycling. It's the difficulty of the terrain, rather than the distance that counts in the outback.

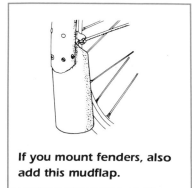

If you mount fenders, also
add this mudflap.

Not something to carry around with you, but this handlebar support is useful for working on the bike. Gene Anthony photo.

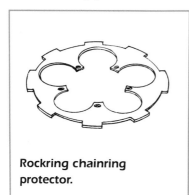

Rockring chainring protector.

Tool kit

Don't leave home for longer trips without the basic tools. Take the time to assemble your personalized tool kit and carry it e.g. tightly rolled up in a rag or a little bag directly under the saddle. See the photograph for the tools you are most likely to need and make sure you check just which types and sizes are needed for your particular bike. Also take some spare parts, spokes, inner tube, chain links and light bulbs and batteries.

Hite-Rite

This is the handy little gizmo that helps in adjusting the seat height quickly and returning it back to its original position. Only needed if you ride in tough and strongly varying terrain — or a theft deterrent to make sure your saddle is not stolen...

'Odds and ends'

There are so many other bits and pieces that it is futile to mention them all here. You can have (plastic) toeclips to keep your feet in place on the pedals (unfortunately, available in only one size: too big). Or handlebar bull-horns to provide a different and better position to hold the mountain bike's straight handlebars. Or a hardened ring to act as a guard for your chainrings so they don't get banged up taking obstacles. Or things that prevent 'chain suck' (i.e. the nasty habit the chain has of get-tiang caught between the rear wheel and the chainstays when you shift down into a lower gear without due care). And new gadgets come out every few months, some to stay, some to disappear into oblivion. Don't buy every gadget you see advertised but talk to people who were stupid (or in very few cases smart) enough to do so to find out whether they really deliver on their promises.

CHAPTER 7

Health and Safety

"You can learn to avoid most of the risks and minimize the impact of these and other injuries or other health hazards."

MOUNTAIN BIKING is not an entirely riskless undertaking. But it is quite possible to reduce the risk to something hardly more than that of staying at home. You can learn to avoid most of the risks and minimize the impact of these and other injuries or other health hazards. That is the subject of the present chapter.

Considering the various risks, ranging from those to your own body and equipment to the harm or loss you may cause others, it may be smart to take out some kind of insurance. Personal liability insurance is perhaps the most important one of these. In addition, you may want to make sure you have adequate health insurance to cover the risk of prolonged treatment if anything serious should happen. These comments of course only apply in such socially archaic societies as the US. My British readers are probably adequately cared for without having to take out their own private insurance.

Important for everyone is to learn how to deal with accidents, injuries, sickness and other health related emergencies while out in the wilds. Do you really know what to do when you are bleeding, when you think you may have broken something, when one of your companions faints or is seriously hurt? Take a first aid course to be prepared for dealing with the unanticipated. That is a lot smarter than shutting your eyes, hoping nothing serious will happen. Even if you are spared yourself, you may be able to save someone else's life. If for one reason or another you can't attend first aid instruction, at least read up on the subject.

The Risks of Mountain Biking

Quite a lot of research has been devoted to bicycle-related accidents and injuries. To summarize the available evidence in a nutshell, the majority of bicycle injuries are attributable to a very limited number of typical mistakes, most of which can be either avoided or counteracted by intelligent cycling techniques.

The risk of falling when mountain biking is always present. Practice catching yourself.
Gene Anthony photo.

The most important lesson to learn from the investigations dealing with the safety of touring cyclists concerns the correlation between risk and trip length. Put simply, the likelihood of getting hurt increases dramatically after many hours in the saddle. That applies especially to cyclists carrying luggage and handling difficult terrain, and most dramatically to inexperienced riders. So don't overextend yourself, and take a break before you get completely exhausted.

Another significant finding is that experienced cyclists have markedly fewer accidents, and can go longer distances before being exposed to the greater risk then those new to the sport. This is one good argument to try and gain experience and skills as quickly as possible. Following the advice contained in chapters 3, 4 and 5 not only increases the joy of riding, it also reduces the risk to which you are exposed.

"Following the advice contained in chapters 3, 4 and 5 not only increases the joy of riding, it also reduces the risk to which you are exposed."

Off-Road 'Traffic' Hazards

Although traffic accidents are the most feared in road biking, they are by no means the only risks of cycling. On the other hand, mountain bikers should not assume that they are immune to them and so need not to concern themselves with the issue: Most mountain bikers finish up riding on roads more than they ever anticipated. Besides, even if you do most of your riding off-road, collisions with other bikers, rangers' trucks, hikers and wildlife on mountain trails have a lot in common with traffic accidents on public roads.

Most accidents of the traffic type simply happen when two people make a mistake each: one initiates a wrong move, and the other fails to react in such a way that a collision is avoided. Keep that in mind when cycling. Remain alert for the possible mistakes others may make, and try to avoid doing the unexpected or unconsiderate yourself as much as humanly possible. Anticipate not only the predictable, but also the unexpected: the ranger's truck looming behind the crest of the hill, the startled deer running across your path, another biker coming your way with his head in the clouds.

In general, ride your bike as you would drive your car, always verifying whether the road or the trail ahead of you is clear, and taking particular care to select your

"As regards riding in traffic, forget anything you ever heard about bikes being different from motor vehicles."

path wisely at junctions and intersections. Before making any move in traffic, look behind you to ascertain that nobody is following closely.

As regards riding in traffic, forget anything you ever heard about bikes being different from motor vehicles. As a wheeled vehicle, your bike is subject to the same laws of physics as your car. Adhere to the most basic rules of traffic, and you'll be reasonably safe on a bike. No doubt the worst advice ever given to cyclists in many parts of the US is to ride on the side of the road where a pedestrian would go, namely facing traffic. On a bike you *are* the traffic, and you belong on the same side as all other vehicles traveling the same way.

In traffic, don't hug the curb but claim your place on the road. Keep at least 90 cm (3 ft) away from the inside edge, even if the road is too narrow to stay clear to the right of the normal path of motor vehicles. Don't dart in and out around parked vehicles and other obstructions along the side of the road.

Falls and Collisions

Virtually every injury to the cyclist results from the impact when the cyclist falls off the bike. He either hits the ground, an object on or along his path, the colliding person, vehicle or animal, or the bike itself. Be watchful, consider the effects of your own actions, and use the technical skills described before to divert when the situation becomes threatening. Four types of falls and collisions can be distinguished: stopping, diverting, skidding and loss of control, as described below.

Develop your riding and handling skills to minimize the risk.
Gene Anthony photos.

"Use the forced turn technique to divert away from danger."

Stopping Accidents

In this kind of collision, the bicycle runs into an obstacle that halts its progress. Depending on the cyclist's speed, the impact can be very serious. As the bike itself is stopped, inertia keeps the rider going forward, throwing him against or over the handlebars. The kinetic energy of the moving mass will be dissipated very suddenly, often in an unfortunate location. Your genitals may hit the handlebar stem or your skull may crash onto something solid.

Guard yourself against these accidents by looking and thinking ahead, so you don't run into any obstacles. If necessary, control your speed ahead of time, to allow handling the unexpected when a potential danger may be looming up behind the next corner. Use the forced turn technique to divert away from danger.

Diverting Accidents

A diverting type accident occurs when the front wheel is pushed sideways by an external force, while the rider is not leaning in the same direction to regain balance. Typical off-road causes are cracks and ridges in the surface. The effect is that you fall sideways and hit the ground or some obstacle by the side of the trail. Depending how unexpectedly it happened, you may be able to break the fall by stretching out an arm.

Typical resulting injuries range from abrasions, lacerations and bruises of the hands and the sides of arms and legs or hips to sprained or broken wrists. More serious cases, usually incurred at higher speeds, may involve broken collarbones and injuries to the face or the side of the skull. The impact of the lesser injuries can be minimized by wearing padded gloves and double layers of clothing with long sleeves and legs. Wearing a helmet will minimize damage to the side of the head.

Diverting accidents can often be avoided if you are careful and alert. Keep an eye out for the typical danger situations. To cross a nearly parallel ridge or gully, use the technique of sideways jumping.

Practice fooling around to learn to handle the bike even in a fall.
H.C. Smolik photo.

Skidding Accidents

When the bicycle keeps going or goes in an unintended direction, despite your efforts to brake or steer, it will be due to skidding between the tires and the ground. This kind of thing typically happens off-road on account of loose gravel or sand, but can also happen on the road due to moisture, frost, loose sand or fallen leaves. Sudden diversions, hard braking and excessive lean when cornering can all cause skidding.

Skidding accidents often cause the cyclist to fall sideways, resulting in abrasions, lacerations or more rarely fractures. Avoid them by checking the road surface ahead and avoiding sudden steering or braking maneuvers and excessive leaning in curves. Cross slick patches with the bicycle upright. Achieve that by carrying out the requisite steering and balancing actions *before* you reach such danger spots.

If you can not avoid it, once you feel you are entering a skid, try to move your weight towards the back of the bike as much as possible, sliding back on the saddle and stretching the arms. Follow the bike, rather than trying to force it back. Finally, don't do what seems an obvious reaction to the less experienced, namely getting off the saddle to straddle the top tube with one leg dangling. As with so many cycling techniques, skidding can be practiced in a relatively safe environment.

Loss of Control Accidents

At higher speeds, especially on steep descents, loss of control accidents sometimes occur. In this case, you just can't steer the bike the way you intend to go. This happens when you have to steer in one direction at a time when you are leaning the other way, or when speed control braking initiates unexpected oscillations. Often this situation develops into a collision or a fall along the lines of one of the accident types described above.

Prevention is only possible with experience: don't go faster than the speed at which you feel in control. The more you ride under various conditions, the more you will develop a feel for what is a safe speed, when to brake and how to steer to maintain control over the bike. Once the situation sets in, try to keep your cool. Don't panic. Follow the bike, rather than forcing it over. The worst thing you can do is to tense up and get off the saddle. Stay in touch with handlebars, seat and pedals, steering in the direction of your lean.

"The worst thing you can do is to tense up and get off the saddle. Stay in touch with handlebars, seat and pedals, steering in the direction of your lean."

Treating Injuries

In the sections that follow, you will get some basic advice on what to do in case of minor injuries. There is of course more to it. Especially if symptoms such as itching or fever occur, you should get professional medical help as soon as possible.

Abrasions

These are the most common cycling injuries resulting from any kind of fall. They usually heal relatively fast, though they can be quite painful. Wash out the wound with water and soap, and remove any particles of dirt to prevent infection. There may be a risk of tetanus if the wound draws blood. If you have been immunized against tetanus, get a tetanus shot within 24 hours only if the last one was more than two years ago. If you have never been immunized before, get a full immunization, consisting of two shot within 24 hours, followed by two more after two weeks and six months, respectively.

Apply a dressing only if the location is covered by clothing, since the wound will heal faster when exposed to the air. Avoid the formation of a scab by treating the wound with an antibacterial cream.

Wear a helmet, gloves and padded clothing to protect yourelf against injury in a fall. H. C. Smolik photo.

Sprained Limbs

In case of a fall, your tendency to stick out an arm to break the impact may result in a sprained wrist. In other accident situations this can also happen to the knee or the ankle. Typical symptoms are a local sensation of heat, itching and swelling.

Whenever possible, keep the area cold with an ice bag (ideal is a pack of frozen peas). If you feel a stinging pain or if fever develops, get medical advice, because it may be a fracture that was at first incorrectly diagnosed.

Fractures

Typical cycling fractures are those of the wrist and the collarbone, both caused when falling — the one when extending the arm to brake the fall, the other when you don't have time to do that. You or medical personnel may not at first notice a 'clean' fracture, i.e. one that is not outwardly visible.

If there is a stinging pain when the part is moved or touched, I suggest you get an X-ray to make sure, even if a fracture is not immediately apparent. You'll need medical help to set and bandage the fractured location, and you must give up cycling until it is healed.

Head Injuries

If you fall on your head, the impact may smash the brain against the inside of the skull, followed by the reverse action as it bounces back. The human brain can usually withstand this kind of treatment without lasting damage only if the resulting deceleration does not exceed about 300 G or 3000 m/sec.

Neither your skull nor the object with which you collide is likely to deform gradually enough to limit deceleration to that value. That's why energy-absorbing helmets with thick crushable foam shells were developed. The crushing of about ¾ inch of seemingly brittle foam is essential to absorb the shock.

Other Health Problems

The remaining part of this chapter will be devoted to the health hazards of cycling that have nothing to do with falling off the bike. We will look at the most common complaints and discuss some methods of prevention, as well as possible cures. This description cannot cover the entire field. Nor should most of the issues discussed here be generalized. The same symptoms may have different causes in different cases; conversely, the same cure may not work for two superficially similar problems. Yet in most cases the following remarks will apply.

Saddle Sores

Try to avoid the most serious seat problems by taking it easy for one or two days when symptoms start to develop. What happens during many hours in the saddle is that the combined effect of perspiration, pressure and chafing causes cracks in the skin where bacteria can enter. The result can be anything from a mild inflammation to the most painful boils.

These things don't heal as long as you continue riding vigorously. As soon as any pressure is applied, when you sit on a bike seat, things get worse again. Prevention and early relief are the methods to combat saddle sores. The main clue is hygiene. Wash and dry both

"The same symptoms may have different causes in different cases; conversely, the same cure may not work for two superficially similar problems."

"In mountain biking, knee problems are easily prevented by using the very low gears available to you."

your crotch and your cycling shorts after every day's ride. Many cyclists also treat the affected areas with rubbing alcohol, which both disinfects and increases the skin's resistance to chafing, or with talcum powder, which prevents further damage.

The quality of your saddle and your riding position may also affect the development of crotch problems. If early symptoms appear in the form of redness or soreness, consider getting a softer saddle, sitting further to the back of your saddle, or lowering the handlebars a little to reduce the pressure on the seat. If the problem gets out of hand, take a rest from cycling until the sores have fully healed

Knee Problems

Because the cycling movement does not apply the high impacting shock loads on the legs that are associated with running, it's surprising that knee problems are so prevalent. Actually, in mountain biking, they are easily prevented by using the very low gears available to you. Pushing too high a gear places excessive forces on the knee joint, resulting in damage to the membranes that separate the moving portions of the joint and the ligaments holding the bits and pieces together. The problem is aggravated in cold weather, so it will be wise to wear long pants whenever the temperature is below 15°C (60°F), especially if fast descents are involved.

Tendinitis

Most typically, this refers to an infection of the Achilles tendon, which attaches the gastrocnemius, the big muscle of the lower leg, to the heel bone. It is an important tendon in cycling, since the pedaling force can not be applied to the foot without it. It sometimes gets damaged or torn under the same kind of conditions as described above for knee injuries: cycling with too much force in too high a gear. This problem, too, is most severe at low temperatures.

To avoid tendinitis, gear low and wear long woollen socks whenever the temperature is below 15°C (60°F). It may also help to wear shoes that come up quite high, maximizing the support they provide. Get used to riding with a supple movement in a low gear, which seems to be the clue to preventing many cycling complaints, including this one.

Numbness

Especially beginning cyclists sometimes develop a loss of feeling in certain areas of contact with the bike. The most typical locations are the hands, but it also occurs in the feet and the crotch. It is caused by excessive and unvaried prolonged pressure on the nerves and blood vessels. The effects are usually relieved with rest, though they have at times been felt for several days.

Don't grip the handlebars too tightly. Once the problem develops, get relief by changing your position frequently, moving the hands from one part of the handlebars to the other, or moving from one area of the seat to the other if the crotch is affected. To prevent numbness from developing in the first place, use well padded gloves, foam handlebar covers, a soft saddle in a slightly higher position and thick-soled shoes with cushioned inner soles, laced loosely at the bottom but tightly higher up.

Back Ache

At high elevations, like here near lake Tahoe at 7,500 ft, sunburn is a problem. Protect your skin or cover up. Gordon Bainbridge photo.

Many riders complain of aches in the back, the lower neck and the shoulders, especially early in the season. These are probably attributable to insufficient training of the muscles in those locations. It is largely the result of unfamiliar isometric muscle work, keeping still in a for-

"After a demanding climb in cold weather, do not strip off warm clothing, open your shirt or drink excessive quantities of cold liquids, even if you sweat profusely."

ward bent position. This condition may also be partly caused or aggravated by low temperatures, so it is wise to wear warm bicycle clothing in cool weather.

To avoid the early-season reconditioning complaints, the best remedy is not to interrupt cycling in winter. Even two longer rides a week at a moderate pace, or extended use of a home trainer with a proper low riding position, will do the trick. Alternately, you may start off in the new season with a slightly higher handlebar position and once more a low gear.

Sinus and Bronchial Complaints

Especially in the cooler periods, many cyclists develop breathing problems, originating either in the sinuses or the bronchi. The same may happen when a rider used to cycling at sea level gets into the mountains, where the cold air in a fast descent can be very unsettling. It's generally attributable to undercooling, the only solution being to dress warmer and to cycle slowly enough to allow breathing through the nose.

After a demanding climb in cold weather, do not strip off warm clothing, open your shirt or drink excessive quantities of cold liquids, even if you sweat profusely. All these things cause more rapid cooling than your body may be able to handle. Cool off gradually and without impairing your health by merely reducing your output and allow the sweat to evaporate naturally through the fibers of your clothing. This works best if you wear clothing that contains a high percentage of wool.

Sunburn

On long rides and at high elevations, you may be exposed to the sun's ultraviolet rays to the point of developing sunburn. To prevent it, use a sun tan lotion with a protection factor of 15 or more. Even more effective is zinc oxide based protection, applied in selected locations such as the nose, the ears and the neck. In severe cases, a sunburn can be serious enough to justify professional medical care. There are substances that suppress the pain, but there is not much in the way of medication that will suppress more than the symptoms, once the damage is done.

CHAPTER 8

Keeping Fit — On and Off the Bike

"Mountain biking can often add the little extra kick of anaerobic work."

Just being outside may be healthy enough for most people. Yet you'll get more out of your mountain biking when you work on your fitness as well.
Gordon Bainbridge photo.

THERE ARE TWO SIDES to the health and fitness coin: On the one hand you can keep fit riding the bike, on the other hand you may become a more proficient mountain biker if you work on your fitness in other respects as well. All forms of cycling are considered excellent endurance sports to build and retain aerobic, or basic cardiovascular, fitness. In addition, mountain biking can often add the little extra kick of anaerobic work that is associated with short duration extremely high output levels. The other aspect has more to do with the need to develop or relax certain muscles to be adequately strong and comfortable on the bike.

Aerobic Fitness

Essentially, aerobic fitness has to do with your heart rate. Cycling for aerobic fitness tends to lower your resting pulse by making the heart strong enough to pump the blood through the veins with fewer, but bigger, strokes per minute. This is presumed to have two positive effects: the heart becomes better equipped to take on increased workloads when needed, and the heart doesn't 'wear out' as fast as it does when you lead a sedentary life.

Whereas aerobic output can be maintained with the oxygen you breathe regularly, anaerobic output levels are those beyond that point and rely on energy stored in the body's blood and muscle tissues. It can be maintained for short periods only and is much more exhausting, leaving you quite depleted afterwards. If you want to enjoy your riding, keep out of this range as much as possible.

To increase or maintain aerobic fitness, all you need do is ride at an extended pace, putting in a real effort continuously for 10 minutes or more each day, or 20 minutes if you train only four days a week. Most riders underestimate the effort needed to achieve a training effect — it is hard work. To establish whether the pace you are riding is adequate, find out what your minimum training pulse should be and make sure you maintain that during the period of exercise. Check your pulse either at the wrist, at the corotid artery (on the side of the neck, just below the jaw), or with a heart rate monitor. Your minimum required training heart rate depends on your age and is most conveniently estimated as follows:

THR = 180 – your age in years

To train effectively for aerobic fitness, follow the following points:

- ☐ Warm up by riding about 10 minutes at a relaxed pace before the actual training session begins.
- ☐ Increase your riding speed gradually over the next couple of minutes, checking your pulse every minute, until the training heart rate is reached.
- ☐ Maintain that output level (but you may have to increase or decrease riding speed to do so, depending

"Most riders underestimate the effort needed to achieve a training effect — it is hard work."

on the terrain) for the required period of 10–20 minutes, depending on the number of times per week you train.

☐ At the conclusion of the training session, ride at a relaxed pace for at least ten minutes to 'warm down,' until you are no longer perspiring, before getting off the bike.

Fit to Ride

Although mountain biking can help you keep fit, it is by no means the ultimate universal exercise routine. In fact, cycling requires some muscles that are not adequately developed by doing so. That may seem like a paradox, but it is inherent in the way some muscles are used in cycling: Isometric muscle work (i.e. keeping the muscle tensioned without it being shortened by the resulting action) essentially does nothing to increase that particular muscle's strength. Consequently, all those muscles of the back, the shoulders, the arms and the

Competition is demanding, and preparing for it will increase your fitness level. Don't forget to relax in between as well.
Gordon Bainbridge photo.

"Weight training should not be used to develop the typical cycling muscles, because riding the bike will take care of that."

For aerobic fitness, it is often more important to ride fast than just to work hard for a short time and then relax again.
Gordon Bainbridge photo.

stomach that are tensed up to restrain your body on the bike don't get any stronger by just riding the bike.

On the other hand, there is the aspect of flexibility. To be comfortable on the bike, to get the tensed-up muscles relaxed and the ones that will be effectively trained adequately flexed and warmed up, you need to do other kinds of exercise. The three techniques used to achieve this are weight training, stretching and gymnastics (or more particularly calisthenics). One final technique is perhaps as important, though it does not do anything to strengthen or flex your muscles: relaxation. The two methods to achieve that are yoga and breathing exercises. This is not the place to find information on yoga, and there are enough books and classes that deal with that, but breathing exercises will be covered below.

Weight training should not be used to develop the typical cycling muscles because riding the bike will take care of that. Instead, it should be used to strengthen the isometrically loaded muscles mentioned above. Rather than give you full instructions on what to do, which would depend too much on just what kind of equipment you are using, simply be conscious which muscles those are. Work on the muscles that ache after a longer ride, i.e. the ones of the arms, shoulders, back, lower arm and stomach, using whatever exercise equipment you choose — dumbbells, stretch bands or a special weight training machine.

Calisthenics and Stretching

These two types of exercise comprise a complex of simple movements to loosen joints and increase the flexibility of muscles. Some of these exercises may also help develop muscles that are not adequately trained by riding the bike. In addition, light exercises of this kind can be useful to loosen and warm up before hard rides. It is presumed to achieve an optimal enzyme activity, necessary for maximum muscle performance, as well as minimizing fatigue. Finally, this kind of work may ease recovery after long-duration hard riding.

The difference between calisthenics (or gymnastics) and stretching lies in the continuity of movement. Each type has its adherents, and my opinion is that a combination of the two forms is best. Certainly when it is cold,

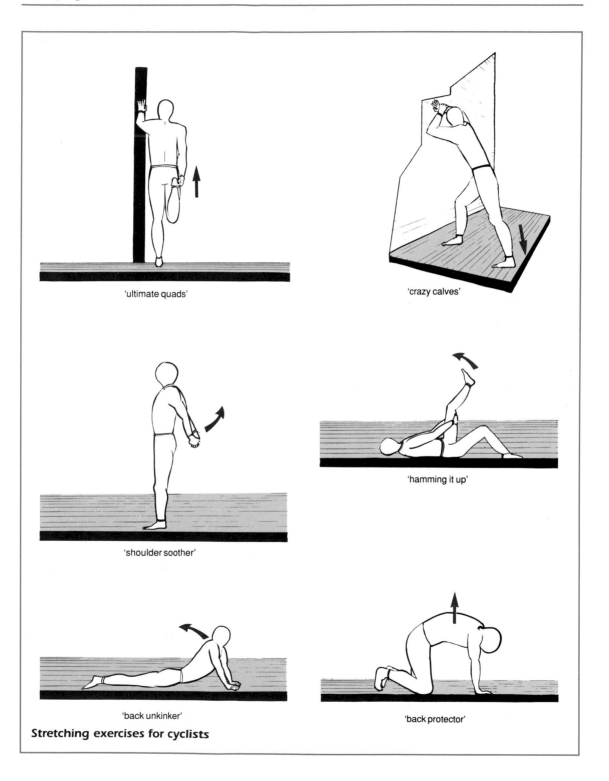

'ultimate quads'

'crazy calves'

'shoulder soother'

'hamming it up'

'back unkinker'

'back protector'

Stretching exercises for cyclists

Keep riding actively in the late and early season for year-round fitness training, and the simple thrills of enjoying nature actively.
Gordon Bainbridge photo.

Efficient breathing technique can have a significant impact on your general feeling of wellbeing and athletic performance.

stretching may do more harm than good. For that reason, I recommend refraining from that kind of exercise outside when the temperatures are low: do calisthenics instead. Even if the air is not cold, your muscles and joints are probably not warm enough when you first start out. Consequently, stretching should always be preceded by some form of warming-up, either cycling, jogging or doing calisthenics. Both calisthenics and stretching exercises are not a substitute for cycling. They merely complement it and improve your physical condition. Specifically, these exercises have the following effects:

☐   Increase movement angles of the joints used in cycling.

☐   Strengthen muscles that are used isometrically in cycling.

☐   Condition the muscles to use a larger range of movement between maximum contraction and maximum extension.

☐   Prevent aches or cramps resulting from tenseness while cycling.

In calisthenics, joints are loosened and muscles conditioned as the body is bent and subsequently stretched in a swinging motion over the greatest joint angle possible (this angle will usually increase significantly with repeated practice).

Of the muscle pairs at any joint, the single muscles that are stretched in calisthenics are strengthened. In stretching, joints and muscles are conditioned to extend fully by forcing them statically in an extremely extended or contracted position, which is reached gradually and then held for at least 30 seconds. On the preceding page, some useful stretching exercises are depicted. These are taken from the book *All Terrain Biking* by Jim Zarka, which covers this subject more thoroughly.

Breathing Exercises

Efficient breathing technique can have a significant impact on your general feeling of wellbeing and athletic performance. In addition to the effect of breathing depth, influencing the amount of oxygen that can be absorbed, there is also an effect on the nervous system: Deep and regular breathing allows the brains to better control movements, reactions, thoughts and emotions, both during exercise and when at rest. The latter effect may well allow the cyclist to divide his powers more effectively, to make more intelligent decisions, and to train more consciously.

Perhaps the simplest and most effective breathing exercise consists of a 20 minute walk at a brisk but regular and unhurried pace, consciously breathing in and out during the same number of steps each time. Start off with cycles consisting of inhalation during 6 steps and exhalation during the next 6 steps. Over the course of several weeks, gradually increase the lengths of these cycles until you are regularly breathing in and out over periods of 9 or 10 steps each. Carried out daily, this exercise is by no means a waste of time that could otherwise be used for more intensive physical training, but builds the foundation for an excellent breathing technique and an unperturbable state of nervous control.

The other essential breathing exercise is equally simple. Breathe in and out several times as deeply as

Total fitness requires more than just biking. You can combine mountain biking in a natural way with other forms of exercise. I can't promise you a figure like this, but I do promise overall fitness if you take every challenge with your mountain bike.
Gene Anthony photo.

Dancing with the bike, during the Black Diamond Mine off-road race in California. Gordon Bainbridge photo.

"The air resistance increases exponentially, resulting in the drastic increase in required power"

possible. When exhaling, try to push the last puff of air out of the farthest corner of the lungs; when inhaling try to take in as much air as your lungs will allow. First do this standing up, bending forward when pushing the air out, raising the upper body fully when breathing in. Follow this by a set of these when lying on the back, keeping the body relatively still. Two sessions daily, comprising perhaps ten respiration cycles each, are adequate to maximize your effective lung capacity. A good time to do breathing work is in between sets of calisthenic exercises or after a moderate-power bout of work on the wind load simulator.

Wind Load Simulator Training

This equipment, also referred to as turbo-trainer, is perhaps the best stationary equipment for bicycle-specific training. It consists of a stand for the bike with a set of rollers that drive wind turbine wheels (or nowadays often electric devices that give the same kind of variable drag that increases with speed). As the speed of the rear wheel increases, either due to faster pedaling in the same gear or to the selection of a higher gear at the same pedaling rate, the air resistance increases exponentially, resulting in the drastic increase in required power typical of cycling at higher speeds under real-world conditions.

Several of these devices can be equipped with a system of air ducts to guide the air that is scooped up by the turbines to discharge a stream of cooling air at the rider's face and chest, which is surprisingly effective. The wind load simulator, especially when equipped with such a cooling system, combines the best possible simulation of real world cycling conditions, with the advantage of being stationary, allowing close monitoring and use under conditions unfavorable to riding the bike.

Mounting an electronic speedometer with additional functions for pedaling speed and pulse rate monitoring provides you with the ultimate in stationary training and monitoring equipment — an exercise physiology lab of your own.

Massage

Although it may not appear to be a training practice, massage has long been recognized as a suitable way of improving both performance and training progress, as well as preventing cramps and injuries. In the context of this book, the most useful remarks on massage will be some guidelines for self-administration. It's nice to have a specialist do it for you, but you can do it yourself quite effectively. Since only *you* can tell how you really feel, this may well be the most effective method anyway.

The most probable justification for massage is the encouragement it provides for the enzyme and blood circulation systems local to the muscles. Another theory holds that in hard, repeated muscle exercise, small fissures are formed and wastes (mainly lactates) accumulate in these fissures within the muscle. Massage is then presumed to encourage the removal of these wastes and to reinstitute a complete flow of blood that can take care of full recovery.

Training together at speed, on a mountain bike tandem. Photo courtesy Gary Fisher MountainBikes.

Whatever the merits of either theory, in practice massage works well and is recommended specifically after particularly long or hard rides. It prevents the 'day after' muscle aches and allows more effective and enjoyable biking.

Procedure for Self-Massage

☐ Take a shower or merely wash the legs in warm (but not hot) water, and dry them thoroughly. There is no real need to use massage oil.

☐ Lie comfortably on your back, at such a distance from the wall that you can stretch your legs above you as shown in the first illustration.

☐ Grab the middle of one of the thighs firmly with both hands, surrounding the muscle bundles; rub forcefully with long, even strokes down from that point towards the hip. Continue this for about one minute.

☐ Now do the same for the section of the thigh from the knee down to the location just beyond where you started under the preceding point. Apply similar regular strokes, continuing for about one minute.

☐ Repeat the work covered in the two prceding points for the other thigh.

☐ Move back from the wall to take the position shown in the second illustration, with the knees bent and the lower leg horizontal.

☐ Carry out a similar massage of the lower legs, working towards the knees, as described above for the thighs.

☐ Briefly massage the muscles of lower and upper legs with about ten long strokes over their entire length.

Afterwards, rest a few minutes, lying on your back with the legs raised, covered with a dry towel if it is cool.

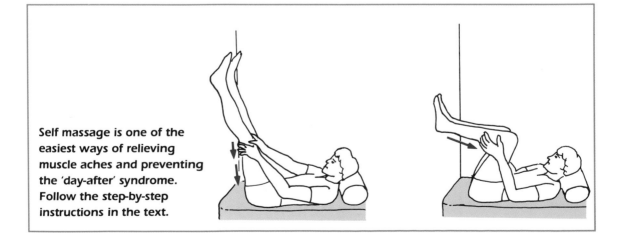

Self massage is one of the easiest ways of relieving muscle aches and preventing the 'day-after' syndrome. Follow the step-by-step instructions in the text.

CHAPTER 9

Getting the Most out of Your Bike

"Consider using the bike for more than purely recreational use only."

THE MOUNTAIN BIKE is not just a fair weather machine for the outback, althought that's one wonderful way to use it: There is much more you can do with it. In this chapter, you will find useful advice on extending the joys of mountain bike riding beyond the limitations of weather and locale. In the first place, you will find it is entirely possible to enjoy mountain biking during seasons that are not commonly considered the best, and within the presumably fair season when the weather is less so. Beyond that, you should consider using the bike for more than purely recreational use only, but for transportation as well.

It is entirely possible to use your mountain bike in the snow. It's just a matter of overcoming limitations. Gordon Bainbridge photo.

Prepare for the Weather

Mountain biking need not be limited to warm and sunny days. Admittedly, it does seem to be more enjoyable to cycle when the weather is nice. However, all seasons have their particular and characteristic charm. Once you learn to cope with bad weather spells, you will probably also find many more opportunities to enjoy the fair weather periods in between.

I grew up in a climate where sunshine and 'real' summer weather are very rare indeed, yet we never hesitated about taking the bike. The first group ride I organized in California, many years later, was a different experience altogether. At seven in the morning the phone rang, with a prospective participant suggesting I call off the ride, since the forecast included a twenty percent chance of rain. Only three of our group of twelve finally showed up for what turned out to be a wonderful ride. Not a drop of rain fell, but even if it should have rained for a while, we would still have had a fine day's ride.

The moral is twofold: don't let uncertainty of the weather stop you from cycling, and prepare well enough to cope with poorer weather, if necessary. Adequately dressed, equipped and prepared, cycling can be enjoyable in almost any weather. Even if we agree that biking is better in favorable weather, and even if you do feel a little miserable at times, a ride in bad weather can still be a lot more enjoyable than sitting at home under the same conditions.

Then there are times of the year or parts of the world for which supposedly bad weather is the order of the day. Of course, it all depends on what you're used to. If you've lived in the American Southwest all your life, you may find it hard to imagine that people a thousand miles north cycle at all, where it even rains in summer, and where it gets pretty cool in the off-season. And what to think of those poor souls who grow up in places like Britain, where even the summers are nippy, and rain can be expected any moment? Learn to handle any kind of weather in order to experience mountain biking as intensely and as frequently as possible. You will probably most enjoy some of the rides in the kind of weather you would at first not have considered suitable.

Four things have to be kept in mind to handle unfavorable weather conditions, which will all be discussed

"Learn to handle any kind of weather in order to experience mountain biking as intensely and as frequently as possible."

in some detail below:

- ☐ clothing
- ☐ other equipment
- ☐ riding style
- ☐ technique

Rough Weather Wear

I shall be brief on the subject of clothing, since it was covered in Chapter 6. The secret is to consciously choose the kind of clothing that suits all the various types of weather you can reasonably expect to encounter on any one ride. In summer, that will include some different things than at other times of the year, and on an extensive tour you will want to be prepared for more changeable conditions than you have to be on a one-day ride.

Also consider the difference of elevation in this respect. I shall not forget one exceptional tour in my own experience that showed me the importance of that. One summer, when I was seventeen years old, long before the

Scott Nicol and Steve Curry caught in a blizzard in the Colorado Rockies.
Gordon Bainbridge photo.

**Dress for the weather, even in sunny areas like California: it can get pretty nippy at times. Below: And sometimes you get caught in the fog.
Photos by Gene Anthony (top) and Gordon Bainbridge (bottom)**

mountain bike was invented, I rode my trusty three-speed from my native city of Rotterdam all the way to the Swiss Alps. At 3000 m (9000 ft) above sea level, I had to put on every fiber I could find and stuff old newspapers under my cycling shirt as well. Even so, I caught an awful cold on the descent.

When packing your gear, decide what range of temperatures and what kind of precipitation you are likely to encounter. Dress for the most immediate, but in such a way that you can convert to another kind of predictable weather without great ado. If rain is likely, make sure the rain gear is easily accessible, and if the temperatures may change, make sure you can accommodate by simply putting on or removing subsequent layers of clothing, rather than being forced to take items off before you can put other ones on. Dressing in layers, with the coolest and lightest closest to the skin, will be best in changeable weather.

On the other hand, if the weather is expected to be and remain cold, you'll find it advantageous to wear warm woollen garments closest to the skin. If additional warm and long underwear is required, remember that your physical activity places specific requirements on your underwear that do not apply to those who are more inactive. Light but slightly bulky fabrics that are flexible and close fitting will be ideal, polypropylene scoring highest when it comes to long underwear.

Not only cold and rain, but even extremely hot or dry weather has to be considered specially. Though it may seem nice to wear as little as possible, keep in mind that you will be out on the bike in the direct sunlight for quite some time. Besides, especially in hilly terrain, sections of great exertion, where your effort keeps you very hot, may be followed by downhill or windy sections, on which your body may get undercooled due to wind chill, even if the air temperature is quite high.

Certainly at higher elevations, I suggest covering up your tender skin. If you haven't a naturally high resistance to ultraviolet rays, wear the kind of cycling clothing that regulates the body's temperature and use an effective sun screen. Refer to Chapter 7 for some additional comments on protection against sunburn. To keep covered enough in the sun without literally melting away, you may wear relatively light cotton items with long sleeves and, of course, a helmet.

To provide the best temperature control effect, wool is definitely the most suitable material, especially if it is closely knit of a relatively thin yarn.

Other Equipment

Cycling in cold or rainy weather is best done on a bike that is equipped with those conditions in mind. That applies even if you encounter such weather only occasionally. On the other hand, the use of removable gadgets, or even some inconvenience in doing without optimal equipment, may be appropriate in some cases. I shall leave it up to you to decide how much suffering you want to put up with. Similarly, it will be a matter of your own inventiveness to produce the handy quick-release attachments and improvised weather protection gadgets that some technically inclined people find a challenge to invent and construct. As for regular equipment to withstand the elements, that will be described in this section.

Particularly in rainy weather, the bike itself must be equipped appropriately. As far as most components are concerned, that means getting high quality gear. To give an example, high quality bearings, as used on the most expensive hubs, bottom brackets and headsets, are much better sealed and more resistant to water than superficially similar items sold for half the price.

The brake blocks should be of any material that provides adequate friction even when wet. Though synthetic materials are widely advertised as being superior in the rain, only one type really lives up to its promise, namely the sintered material used by Modolo and now available in a version that fits some other makers' brakes. Contrary to popular prejudice, longer or larger brake blocks do not provide better braking action than short ones — whether wet or dry.

In wet and cold times of the year, you will probably more often find the need for lighting on your bike. This subject was covered in Chapter 6. Make sure lights and reflectors are properly installed and maintained, and switch on your light whenever other road users' visibility may be impaired enough to justify lighting. In wet and snowy weather, a generator may more easily slip off the tire, and a battery may get soaked and ruined; so check

"High quality bearings, as used on the most expensive hubs, bottom brackets and headsets, are much better sealed and more resistant to water than superficially similar items sold for half the price."

A mountain bike derivative with bells and whistles. This dressed up mountain bike for the European market is highly suitable for everyday use. Renner photo.

up on these components more frequently. Proper adjustment and removing batteries when not in use will prevent the most serious problems.

Other equipment-related points include a more frequent need for bike maintenance and the installation of some auxiliaries that may not otherwise rate very high. Lubrication is the major consideration here: cables, bearings and especially the chain will need regular cleaning, followed by lubrication, using a waxy spray can lubricant, oil or grease. Amongst special equipment, fenders, or mudguards, rate high, as does a mudflap at the end of the forward one, to keep the water off your body, especially your feet. In weather that is both wet and cold, a pair of shoe covers on the pedals are very worthwhile.

Riding Style

In cold, windy and rainy weather, you may benefit from an appropriate riding style. Try to become aware of the effect any particular condition may have on your bike's behavior. In the rain, you'll want to ride so as to stay as comfortable as possible, while retaining maximum stability and balance. In cold weather, you'll want to avoid exposing yourself too much and — when temperatures get down to freezing — you should make sure you don't skid on ice or snow. In very windy weather, it will make sense to minimize your exposure to the wind, so as to reduce wind resistance and minimize the negative effect of the wind on your bike's balancing. The latter applies particularly in the case of a strong side wind, especially if the wind or its effect varies strongly during the ride.

To avoid spills on wet, muddy or icy surfaces, adjust your center of gravity to center minimal weight over the front wheel. The more weight you transfer from the front wheel to the back, the less likely a sudden move will be to result in a skidding or diverting type of disturbance, as described in Chapter 7. For the same reason, try to avoid excessive lean in corners: ride a natural, rather than a forced curve whenever possible. Read through the explanation in Chapter 4 again and practice the techniques recommended there on dry and wet surfaces to become really competent and confident.

"Become aware of the effect any particular condition may have on your bike's behavior."

In windy situations, keep your upper body low, in order to minimize wind resistance. When riding in a group on wider trails or public roads, try to stay in some such formation that minimizes the individual rider's total exposure to the wind. That's done by riding directly in line closely behind each other when the wind comes from straight ahead. In the case of a side wind, fan out the group into a staggered formation. The strongest rider should maximize his time in the front, while the weaker ones should be granted maximum shelter. If all are more or less equally strong, take turns at the front.

Special biking techniques may be called for in inclement weather, although some people manage to solve all their problems by merely wearing appropriate clothing and having a properly equipped bike. One of the things to keep in mind is the long-term chilling effect, due to relative air movement, even if the temperatures do not seem quite so low. Keep especially your extremities warm and comfortable: feet, hands and head.

On longer trips there is spare clothing and other gear to consider. Whenever the weather is or may become sub-optimal, you should have packed everything in such a way that vital items remain dry and are accessible without getting wet — including especially those things on which you have to rely later to keep you dry, warm and comfortable. That's a matter of packing and wrapping your equipment and luggage with due consideration. It is not possible to give you precise guidelines on how to do it, but a warning to consider these points should suffice the intelligent rider.

The way you plan the overall tour or the day's ride is also critical. In certain kinds of weather, you won't be able to cover big distances between stops. At other times, getting off the bike frequently may actually make the ride more uncomfortable. In an enduring rain, you will probably find it beneficial to attack the day as much as possible in just one or two long continuous stretches. By the time you are changed and getting about off the bike, you will be grateful if you don't have to start all over again after the interruption.

In particularly cold weather you should probably ride several shorter sections. Try to find a warm and sheltered place and something warm to eat or drink between these stages. Don't return to the bike until you feel comfortable. Though I shall probably never enjoy cold

Dipped in mud. This mountain bike went through the rainy season. Clean it after every ride if it gets this dirty, so it is ready for the next ride.
H. C. Smolik photo.

In wet weather, you can expect to run into situations like these occasionally. This crossing at the bottom of the famed Repack run in California is perfectly dry most times of the year. Gordon Bainbridge photo.

weather myself, I have at times covered quite significant distances this way without getting really miserable. Some people actually enjoy a brisk ride in the cold, and cover quite impressive distances without either harm or discomfort.

Using the Mountain Bike for Transportation

Don't just ride your bike in search of fun: Try to extend the fun by using the bike as much as you can. The post office, the bank and the library, even the theater and your place of work, are perfect targets for bike trips. I shall not go into details here, but it is only through frequent and universal use of the bike that you become really at ease with the machine. You'll get a lot more miles of biking practice — and you'll enjoy every minute of it.

As a first step, ride your bike to the trail head whenever you can. Anything up to five or six miles on the road can be handled on the bike as quickly as in a car. You save the time loading and unloading the bike and finding places to park the car. Besides, it is environmentally and socially a lot more responsible to minimize car traffic.

Using the bike for transportation means more often riding in traffic, although your mountain bike will offer you plenty of opportunities for shortcuts or detours around some of the main roads. Whenever you ride in traffic, do so as though you were riding a car, not as though your bike answered to the same rules as pedestrians. Don't hug the outside curb but claim your lane, riding determinedly in the middle of it and only moving over to let faster vehicles pass when *you* decide it is safe. Take particular care at intersections to take the correct path well before the actual intersection, so you are not cut off: from the middle of the lane to go straight, from the RH side to turn right and from the LH side of the lane to turn left, looking behind you and signalling early.

CHAPTER 10

Mountain Bike Touring

"Bike touring has been revolutionized by the introduction of the mountain bike."

BICYCLE TOURING is defined as multi-day bike trips over longer distances with overnight stays. This form of recreation has been revolutionized by the introduction of the mountain bike. Not only has the mountain bike itself almost completely taken over as the machine of choice for those who tour, also the routes you can take when touring by bike have changed as a result: you are no longer restricted to asphalt. In this chapter, you will find guidelines for the selection of equipment for touring, for the way to pack the bike and for how to plan and carry out your tour.

The mountain bike is the ideal vehicle for exotic tours to places where the road ends. Dieter Glogowski photo.

Choice of Equipment

Your mountain bike itself is probably suitable for touring the way it came from the shop. As long as it has bosses, or braze ons, for water bottles and luggage racks, you are well on your way. Install racks both front and rear, since it is better to distribute the load more evenly. Make sure you choose racks that are sturdy and match the locations of the bosses and eyelets on your bike. For the front, 'low-rider' racks are the most suitable, distributing the load as shown in the middle detail of the illustration.

If you will be touring at night and in wet regions of the world, the addition of lights and fenders will be called for. Since you won't have many opportunities to recharge batteries underway, use disposable batteries rather than rechargeable ones. If you prefer generator, or dynamo, lighting, get the metal roller replaced by a 1 inch diameter rubber wheel, which makes much better contact. Adjust it to contact the side of the rim rather than the tire, which greatly reduces resistance.

"Your mountain bike itself is probably suitable for touring the way it came from the shop."

Touring with a light load in the Swiss Alps. Renner photo.

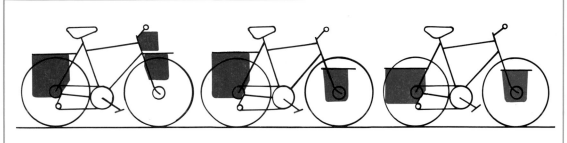

Luggage distribution methods: use the method shown in the middle for maximum stability.

Packing the Load

"Don't just go for the optics but for practicality."

There is a wide selection of bicycle bags available and it should not be hard to find some that appeal to you. Don't just go for the optics but for practicality. The openings must be big and the closures designed to cover them up with a generous overlap. Drawstring designs have the advantage that they are compact when half full as well as when completely stuffed. The best material is not some modern coated synthetic but old fashioned duck or canvas. These natural fibers are hygroscopic, soaking up just enough water in the rain to swell and seal the contents of the bag against penetrating water, whereas none of the synthetics are really adequately waterproof at the seams.

To make it suitable for long distance touring, you need racks and suitable bags — and a big water canister if you happen to be crossing the desert. A 'conservative' frame geometry, rather than one of the super agile competition models now popular, is ideal. Dieter Glogowski photo.

Check stability of load by shaking packed bike sideways.

Pack the various bags with due consideration. Put things that belong together in the same bag, and put stuff that you need first or quickly close to the outside. Put raingear in an outside pocket, so the rest of your luggage does not get wet while you get it out. Make sure the bags you use in the front are evenly packed so they are about equally heavy on both sides (this is much less critical in the rear). Keep the handlebar bag as lightly packed as possible and use it only for things you need regularly and those of value, since it is the only bag you can take with you when you leave the bike.

Pack the bags on the bike itself in such a way that the load is reasonably divided and the bags are firmly attached. The bags must all be tied down to the bike at the bottom as well as at the top. To attach bags other than those with integral attachments, don't use bungee cords but webbing straps or leather belts with buckles.

Planning the Tour

While touring, you may have to get ready for some surprises, such as this ford crossing.
Gordon Bainbridge photo.

Start planning your tour well ahead of time. It not only makes the experience more predictable and less frustrating, it also extends the pleasure to the time of preparation. Once you have decided on the general location, decide how to get there and buy detailed maps of the area as well as a guidebook to find out what the points of interest are and what kind of conditions to anticipate. Study these with your particular purpose in mind. Get fully acquainted with the maps and their legend, so you can interpret them quickly and accurately out in the field.

The best scale for the maps used depends on the purpose and the terrain. To do a rough overall plan for a long tour, especially if you will mainly be using roads, a regular motoring map at a scale like 1:500,000 is probably good enough. For detailed planning when touring by road, 1:200,000 is fine, but for off-road cycling, you will need a scale of 1:25,000 or 1:50,000. In the US, the US Geological Survey, the Bureau of Land Management and various federal and state agencies have suitable maps that can all be obtained at specialized map stores or at the USGS offices in a number of cities. In Britain, only the 1:50,000 Ordnance Survey maps are detailed enough for real off-road cycling.

A primitive crossing (above), and camping out in the desert. Dieter Glogowski photos.

Once you have selected your general route, make sure it can be divided up into bite-sized portions for each day, reaching a location suitable for an overnight stay. The distance you can cover in a day depends very much on the terrain. For touring on regular roads, 60–70 miles (90–110 km) is generally a safe maximum, giving you about 5 hours of cycling and enough time for meals, snacks, breaks and taking care of other needs along the way. Under off-road conditions, it is probably safe to halve these figures: A 35 mile off-road tour can be quite a challenge, even though the distance seems modest. If you mix sections of off-road riding with road use, the distance will lie somewhere in between.

Although the mountain bike does well on hills, the best route to select still remains the most level one possible. You'll have a lot of miles to cover and it makes no sense to waste energy going up when you could be going forward instead. Many times, a detour around a steep hill will save you time and energy, because 300 ft of elevation difference corresponds to as much as one

Mailing a letter home from Nepal.
Dieter Glogowski photo.

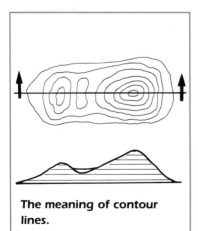

The meaning of contour lines.

linear mile on level ground. Use maps with contour lines (brown lines connecting points at the same elevation) and choose your route in such a way that you cross as few of them as possible, following the contours whenever possible instead.

Decide whether you will be camping out each time or will have either frequent or occasional opportunities to seek shelter in hotels or motels. Although that may not seem like the ultimate outdoor experience, it can be very convenient and is often possible by choosing your route just a little differently, to return to the back country the next day. Get a small notebook in which you write all your planning information, from the selected route and the details of your travel connections to your packing lists.

Before the actual tour, try out all your equipment. The best way to do so is by going on a weekend camping trip not too far from home, trying to replicate the actual conditions of your tour as much as possible. You'll be astonished how many things you'll decide to do differently, how many things you would have forgotten, and how many things you could have left home. Take notes of these and correct the pertinent lists in your notebook to make sure you don't waste time and effort on the actual tour.

Inform at least one acquaintance about your plans. Not just casually, but leave hima day-to-day itinerary

"The best time to plan the details for any day's ride is the night before."

and make a firm commitment to keep him informed about your whereabouts during the trip. Put them in charge of checking with you and informing safety patrols in the area where you are touring when you do not report as planned. Your own responsibility will be to report to this person exactly as planned and keep him informed about any changes in your itinerary, either before or after your departure. This way, if anything should go wrong, all the pertinent information will be available to search for you and bring in help quickly and accurately.

Probably nothing will go wrong, but it helps if you are prepared for the worst. Once you get back home, record your experiences in the notebook, making specific comments about the things to watch out for or do differently on any subsequent tour and modifying your packing lists as appropriate. Put your experiences to work for you by consulting these notes before your next tour.

Executing the Tour

During the tour, try to follow your own plans as closely as possible. These plans don't necessarily include turning left at this intersection and going straight at the next, but should at least outline the bigger steps, so each day you reach your predetermined goal. The best time to plan the details for any day's ride is the night

Not everybody's idea of having a good time: the Alaska Iditabike tour. Those who've done it loved it — they say. Renner photo.

Waterfront touring in the Sierras.
Gordon Bainbridge photo.

before, when you are best informed about the general local conditions and your own condition. Lay out your route on the map with a marking pen and estimate how long it will take to reach certain intermediate goals.

While riding, consult your map constantly. Don't wait until you are lost before getting the map out, because that way you'll not even be able to establish where you might be, much less how to get back on the right track. If the worst comes to the worst, retrace your ride back to the last point where you were last certain of your correct location and start again from there, paying better attention as you go this time.

Each time possible, make your call to the contact person and tell him not only that you have safely reached your planned destination for the day, but also what kind of problems you have had, and any change of your plans for the next days. All this may sound exaggerated, but it takes a lot of worry off you in case anything unexpected happens. Again, usually nothing goes wrong, but it is a relief just to be able to confirm it.

CHAPTER 11

Mountain Biking for Competition

"Mountain Bike racing is now an officially sanctioned sport and international competition is growing."

Competitors struggle their way through a difficult section at the NORBA Nationals near Santa Barbara.
Gordon Bainbridge photo.

LONG BEFORE the mountain bike was a commercially available commodity, mountain biking was a sport, and a somewhat casual but nonetheless pretty competitive sport at that. Today's mountain bikes trace their lineage back to the modified clunkers with which California and Colorado daredevils threw themselves down the steep barren hillsides to see who could do it the fastest, later expanded to get back up the slope on the bike as well. Since those days, mountain bike racing has developed greatly. It is now an officially sanctioned sport in the US and international competition is growing, with World Championships drawing heavy publicity.

Coming down fast at the Black Diamond Mine Race in Clayton, California Gordon Bainbridge photo.

"NORBA regularly sanctions races for all categories, ranging from novices and juniors to experts and professionals, for men and women alike."

Today, the sport has become much more structured and even takes on international dimensions. The Europeans regularly compete on the international level throughout the season for the Grundig cup, and the annual World Championships pits the best of Europe against the best riders from North America.

But you don't have to be of World Championship caliber to compete in mountain biking. In the US, NORBA, the National Off-Road Bicycle Association which is now operated by the United States Cycling Federation, regularly sanctions races for all categories, ranging from novices and juniors to experts and professionals, for men and women alike. Unlike most other sports, women's off-road racing is actually taken very seriously, with big money and publicity for the best amongst the pros.

The wonderful thing about most mountain bike races is the fact that the events for novices are held in the same place and on the same day as those for pros and experts. This way, you can measure your own progress against that of the best in the sport and compare their techniques for handling certain obstacles with yours.

To participate in any kind of off-road racing, you need a license, but that is often easier to obtain than it is in most other sports. In most countries, you don't even have to be a member of the sanctioning organization just to try it out for a few races: At a modest fee, you can get a one-time license valid for the particular event and delay your membership and official licensing until you are sure off-road racing is really what you want to do. The need for licensing is apparent if you consider the intricacies of getting access to racing sites and the liabilities involved — you will be insured for the duration of the event and when you join and get a regular license, the insurance will cover you while training or participating in casual competition as well.

"In most countries, you don't even have to be a member of the sanctioning organization just to try it out."

Observed trials competition is a great test of handling skills. No speed and cheap thrills here. Shown here is Andy Grayson, performing at Briones Park in California. Gordon Bainbridge photo.

Types of Races

As in most other athletic pursuits, there are quite a number of different disciplines in off-road racing as well. The oldest form is the simple downhill race: see who gets to the bottom of the hill the fastest. The uphill is often ridden over the same terrain but requiring that you follow a different course part or all the way due to the steepness and lack of traction in certain sections that make the downhill a challenge but climbing impossible.

Both these events are typically of relatively modest length and duration: less than a mile. At least the downhill is usually ridden as a time trial, with riders starting individually at one-minute intervals. Combining downhill and uphill sections into a single race results in an uphill-downhill, and either the times are cummulated or riders are awarded points on the basis of their placings in each part.

Challenges and enduros are the more typical round course races that are similar to what is ridden in the established bike racing discipline of cyclo-cross. But unlike cyclo-cross, mountain bike challenges are mainly ridden, even though there is no restriction against walking and carrying the bike over certain difficult sections. The mountain bike is designed to be ridden, whereas the cyclo-cross bike is designed to be carried. But there is a technique of carrying the mountain bike as well without losing much time.To do that, coast down to walkin speed ready to dismount on the LH side, then slide the RH arm through the frame, raising the bike on your shoulder while grabbing the handlebars with the right hand — all done while continuing to run.

An entirely different kind of off-road event is known as observed trials and has its roots in the kind of motorcycle racing in which not speed but skill is the criterion. A very difficult course is ridden and the skill is to get through it without getting a foot on the ground. This is the most skill-intensive form of off-road competition.

The introduction of front suspension, such as this Rock Shox fork, has greatly influenced the downhill racing scene.
Photos courtesy manufacturer (top) and H. C. Smolik (bottom).

Equipment

The mechanical equipment used for racing is not really that different from what you and I can buy in the shop. There are few secrets that really warrant getting a very special bike, and until such time that you are discovered by a sponsor who thinks you can do well to promote his product, there is little or nothing to be gained from spending excessive money on very special gear. Any reasonably light and well made mountain bike will see you through most races.

Certain events are best ridden with their characteristics in mind. Thus, for downhill events, a bike with a long wheelbase and a steady character, even if it is a little heavy, will be fine. Adding a suspension, such as the Rock-Shox sprung front fork or even a sprung frame, will give you maximum advantage in this kind of event.

For uphill riding, short wheelbase bikes are generally best, providing you have learned to handle them by shifting your balance back and forth to keep traction on the one hand and steering control on the other. Weight counts more on the uphill of course, so if climbing is your specialty, a lightweight bike should be the thing to get.

Uphill-downhills and challenges or enduros ought to be ridden on the same bike, even if the ultimate for the downhill is not the same as for the uphill sections. I very much favor outlawing changing bikes during all mountain biking events, and hope the UCI, the international cycling federation, sees fit to include such a ruling. This

Fast cornering in a downhill time trial.
Renner photo.

Coming down a difficult and narrow stretch at the Great Flume Race in the High Sierras. Gordon Bainbridge photo.

"When training, concentrate on whatever you are doing. Ride all out for continuous stretches at least as long as the actual event."

way, it becomes not a battle to see who can afford the biggest number of different bikes, but one to see who has the smartest combination of riding skills and judgment to chose the gear that best sees him or her through all sections of mixed terrain.

Special bikes have been developed for the noble sport of observed trials. With small wheels, small frame, high bottom bracket and adjustable brakes, some of these bikes almost resemble BMX Freestyle machines, from which they indeed borrow some of the components. But whatever the bike used for this sport, the skills are ones that can be practiced on any mountain bike. Just make sure you practice them on the particular bike you'll be using well before the event because these bikes take some getting used to, although they can let you do things you can't do with a regular mountain bike.

Training for Off-Road Racing

Preparing for any kind of competition requires three things: physical training, skills development, and tactical insight. Obviously, it will be impossible to cover all the techniques used to achieve that in the context of just one chapter of a general book like this.

The basic advice is simple enough though, and will see you through a first season of racing: Always ride with the intent to enter in competition in mind. Concentrate on whatever you are doing. Ride all out and long continuous stretches at least as long as the actual events you plan to participate in to build strength and endurance. Practice and apply all the skills described in the early chapters of this book: Rather than getting off to go around a puddle or a log, make a habit of negotiating them while staying on the bike. And think of what you are doing and how you would handle certain situations if you were to encounter them in a race to hone your racing tactics.

Build up your physical fitness given in Chapter 8, following all the advice on stretching and other exercises. Before and after training rides get into the habit of warming up and warming down, respectively. Practice self-massage to keep your muscles toned and to aid recovery. Be conscious of what and how you eat: go easy on fat and sugar. Keep your weight under control by checking your weight changes against your eating habits regularly. The day before a race, don't eat your main meal too late in the day (at least 4 hours before going to bed).

The day of the actual race, have your last solid meal (mainly carbohydrates) at least two hours before the start. On hot days and longer duration rides, drink water or fruit juice before the race, and if the course takes more than an hour, take a drink on the bike and sip something at least every fifteen minutes. Only on very long races and training rides will you need nutrition during the ride, for which things like Power Bars and dried fruit are ideal.

As in so many other pursuits as well, racing is best learned by doing it. You can read up on it and even exercise a lot without gaining much unless you put it into practice first. So enter a race at the earliest possible stage, assuming you are at least fit enough to complete the course at any speed. If you are at all like me, your first experience will be very disheartening unless you are

In the conventional sport of cyclo-cross, drop handlebar racing bikes have been traditionally used. In recent years, more and more riders have introduced the mountain bike in this discipline as well, often with considerable success. Here John Loomis at a cyclo-cross race in Santa Barbara, California. Gordon Bainbridge photo.

Going fast at a Grundig Cup race in southern Germany. Andreas Schlüter photo.

aware that a lot is gained by the hands-on experience gained in actual participation. After the race, don't take off with your tail between the legs, but stick around and talk to the other participants to learn a thing or two.

The first day after a race, take it easy, but the next day, get back on the bike and start practicing what you've found out you were doing wrong — or merely not well enough. Work on your weak points to improve them and on your strong points to maximize the advantages they bring you. After participating in half a dozen events, especially if you can find other racers to practice with, your performance will mysteriously improve and you will enjoy the sport to the fullest.

CHAPTER 12

Maintaining the Mountain Bike

"Keep your mountain bike in optimum condition to enjoy the use of a trouble-free bike even after years of use."

IT MAKES SENSE to keep your mountain bike in optimum condition to enjoy the use of a trouble-free bike even after years of use. If you do ride off-road a lot, especially if you don't restrict yourself to fair-weather riding, your machine will get dirty and it will get knocked about more than a regular road bike does.

With the advice in this chapter, you will be able to keep it working reliably and predictably for a long time. You can even make it look halfway respectable, so you are not so easily tempted to blame the bike when you're not performing as well as you think you should. In this chapter, I shall cover cleaning the bike, adjustments, pre-

When working on the bike, it is best to support it on a work stand. If you must rest it upside down, make sure you use something to support the handlebars off the ground, so as not to damage the shifters and the cables.

All photos in this chapter by Gene Anthony.

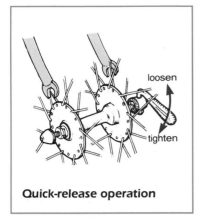

Quick-release operation

ventive maintenance, and simple repairs. In addition to real maintenance work, the mechanics of adjusting and removing handlebars, saddle, wheels and pedals are described here too.

Quick-Release Operation

Whether on the saddle or the wheels, the mountain bike's quick-releases are operated the same way. When the lever is twisted from the open to the closed position, an excentric cam at the end where it is held on the spindle or bolt on the lever locks the connection tight.

The secret is not to try and use the lever like a wing nut. Instead, just cock or uncock it by twisting it one direction or the other. If you don't notice a definite resistance and locking action, tighten the thumbnut at the other end a little while the lever is in the open position. If you can't move the lever all the way over, loosen the thumbnut a little, again with the lever in the open position.

Cleaning the Bike

Saddle adjustment with quick-release binder bolt.

You don't just need a clean bike to show it off — nor do you need a dirty bike to show off that you do a lot of riding. Clean bikes are easier to adjust and maintain. Make a habit of cleaning it regularly, like once a week. All you need is three rags, one or two brushes (soft bushy round paint brushes and one or two different size bottle brushes) some water and once or twice a season, car wax. Now follow the relevant steps below, depending on the state of the bike;

1. Brush all the loose dirt off the bike, working your way into all the nooks and crannies with the brushes, except where the greasy dirt has collected.

2. Using water and either a sponge or one of the rags, clean the caked-on dirt off the bike. Although it will be necessary to get water into hidden corners, avoid getting it into the bearings. That is one of the reasons I'd rather use a bucket of water and a rag than a hose (the other reason being the need to conserve water where I live).

3. Your first rag is now somewhat dirty, and you can

"Use car wax on all the blank metal parts and the paint to preserve it. Wax dries hard and does not attract dirt as grease does."

use it to clean the locations where greasy dirt has accumulated.

4. Dry the whole bike with the third rag, which should still be clean and dry.

5. If appropriate, use car wax on all the blank metal parts and the paint to preserve it. Wax is much better to use than greasy substances such as vaseline, because it dries hard and does not attract dirt as grease does. Shine the whole bike up with the clean, dry rag.

6. Once a season, precede the waxing operation by touching up any scratched paint. If you did not get any touch-up paint with the bike (it should be supplied but rarely is), look for a matching paint at any model shop. If the metal is exposed, sand it down, if not, just clean the spot with paint thinner or turpentine. Use a very fine brush or a broken matchstick to apply the paint only where the old paint has been removed, trying not to overlap. Let dry 24 hours before using the bike, and at least a week before waxing it.

Inspection and Lubrication

Carry out the most basic inspection of the bike each day, or before every ride: are the tires inflated to the appropriate pressure for the terrain, are handlebars and saddle firmly in place at the right height, do the brakes and the gears work properly? At least once a month, check for a few more points:

☐ *Wheels:* Do they turn perfectly round, without wobbling, and are the spokes all tensioned the same?

☐ *Tires:* Are they free from cuts and embedded sharp objects?

☐ *Brakes:* Do the brake pads touch the rims over their entire length, and only the rims?

☐ *Frame and forks:* Is any damage, such as bulges in the tubes just behind the headset, or bent fork blades or drop-outs apparent?

☐ *Drivetrain:* Does the chain run smoothly as you turn the cranks forward and back, shifting between all the gears?

The brakes must be adjusted so they can be applied fully without the levers 'bottoming out.'

Lubricate the points marked with an arrow.

Adjusting the brake cable

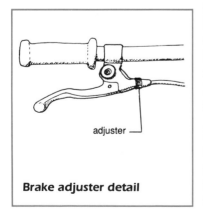

Brake adjuster detail

☐   *Bearings:* Can you detect any play in the bearings of pedals, wheel hubs, headset and bottom bracket?

Lubrication:

Lubricate the pivot points shown in the illustration, using a spray lubricant and wiping any excess off afterwards. Although the bearings also require occasional lubrication, that should not be done with the spray lubricant but with bearing grease. Since this work usually requires disassembly of the bearings, it may be the kind of work to leave to a bike shop. Get it done at least once a year — more frequently if you ride in very dusty or wet conditions a lot.

Maintenance

The simplest and most frequent maintenance and repair jobs are explained below. If any of the other things are seriously wrong, you are best advised to take the bike to a bike shop and get the specific problem fixed. If you are into doing things like that yourself (highly recommended, because an understanding of such basic maintenance jobs is of benefit when anything happens while you are riding), learn to do it yourself with the aid of a bicycle repair book, e.g. my *Mountain Bike Maintenance.*

Brake Maintenance

To make sure the brakes work properly, try them out separately at walking speed, which is perfectly safe and still gives a representative test of the deceleration reached with each brake. Used alone while riding the bike on level ground, the rear brake must be strong enough to skid the wheel when applied firmly. The front brake should decelerate the bike so much that the rider notices the rear wheel lifting off when it is applied fully. If their performance is inadequate, carry out the adjustment described in the next section.

Brake Adjustment

Usually, the brake must be adjusted because its performance is insufficient. In this case, the cable tension has to be increased by decreasing its effective length. Should the brake touch the rim even when not engaged, the op-

Releasing the brake's straddle cable.

posite must be done to lengthen the cable slightly.

Before starting, check to make sure the brake blocks lie on the rim properly over their entire width and length when the brake is applied. Ideally, the front of the brake block should touch the rim just a little earlier than the back. If necessary, adjust by loosening the brake block bolt, moving the block as appropriate. Retighten it while holding the brake block in the right position. If necessary, the brake block may be replaced, after which it must be adjusted as well.

Adjusting procedure

1. Release the nipple of the brake straddle cable.
2. Loosen locknut on the adjusting mechanism.
3. While holding the locknut, screw the barrel adjuster out by several turns; then hook the straddle cable nipple in place again.
4. Check the brake tension: the brake must grab the rim firmly when a minimum of 2 cm ($^3/_4$ in) clearance remains between the brake handle and the handlebars.
5. If necessary, repeat steps 1—4 until the brake works properly.
6. Tighten the locknut again, while holding the adjusting barrel to stop it from turning.

Derailleur Maintenance

The indexed derailleur systems used on the modern mountain bike work very well, but once they get out of adjustment, they can be quite frustrating, especially if you have one on which the shifter cannot be set from the indexed to the friction mode. When the gears no longer engage properly, adjust the cable tension using the barrel adjuster at the derailleur or at the shifter to correct the problem, following this procedure:

1. Put the shifters in the position for the front derailleur to engage the smallest chainring, for the rear derailleur to engage the smallest sprocket and turn the cranks until they are indeed engaged.
2. Check to make sure the cables are neither slack nor tensioned at this point. Adjust by turning the adjuster in or out as required to correct cable tension.

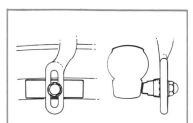

The brake pads must touch the rims over their entire length and width.

Derailleur adjustment, either on the shifter or on the derailleur itself, depending on the model in question.

3. Shift to the middle chainring in the front and check all the gears with the rear derailleur. If they don't engage properly, readjust the cable tension for the rear derailleur only by tightening it half a turn at a time. If no improvement is apparent after two full turns, return to the original position and try loosening in steps of half a turn at a time.

4. Once the rear derailleur has been adjusted properly, place it in the position for one of the middle gears and repeat the same procedure for the front derailleur, adjusting the cable tension for it until the three chainrings can all be engaged properly.

Note:

If you have no luck with this adjustment, see your bike shop.

Drivetrain Maintenance

The cranks are held on the spindle by means of a bolt, covered by a dust cap in the crank. This method of attachment is referred to as *cotterless*. On a new bike, the cranks tend to come loose after some use, as they may at more infrequent intervals later on. For this reason, and for other maintenance or replacement work, I suggest you obtain a matching crank tool for the particular make and model installed on your bike. Check and tighten the cranks every 25 miles during the first 100 miles, and perhaps once a month afterwards.

Tighten Cotterless Crank

1. Remove the dust cap with any fitting tool (on most models a coin may be used).

2. Using the wrench part of the special crank tool, tighten the recessed bolt firmly, countering at the crank.

3. Reinstall the dust cap.

Chain Maintenance

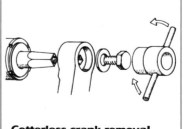

Cotterless crank removal or tightening detail.

The chain connects the crankset with the rear wheel, where a freewheel block with several different size sprockets is installed. The chain is routed around the sprocket and both derailleur wheels so it is kept tensioned. It should neither hang loose nor tighten up ex-

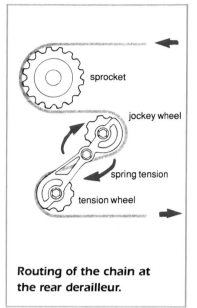

Routing of the chain at the rear derailleur.

cessively when using either of the extreme gearing combinations (big chainring with the biggest sprocket or small chainring with the smallest sprocket).

An endless chain is used, which may be parted by removing one of the pins connecting two links. The same method is used to add or remove links to adjust the chain's length. It may be necessary to remove the chain for cleaning and lubrication. Wash it out in solvent and lubricate it using a spraycan with a waxy or silicon-based lubricant. To remove or part the chain, you will need a chain tool, following the following procedure:

Chain Removal and Installation

1. Put the chain on a combination of a small chainwheel with a small sprocket, to release its tension.
2. Place the tool on one of the pins connecting two links, and turn it in by 6 turns.
3. Turn the handle of the tool back out and remove the tool from the chain.
4. Wriggle the chain apart.
5. Reinstall the chain, routing it around the derailleur as shown in the illustration.

Wheel removal or installation (shown with quick-release).

Wheel Maintenance

The jobs that occasionally need doing on the wheels include replacing a broken spoke, wheel truing (which is done to return the thing to its proper shape after it got bent) and fixing a flat.

Wheel Removal and Installation

For most of these things, you will have to remove the wheel. To do so, simply use the quick-release, but first undo the brake by unhooking the nipple of the straddle cable that connects the two brake arms, so the tire can pass by the brake blocks.

The quick-release (just like the one on the saddle) should be used correctly: Don't treat the lever like something to thread in or out; instead, just cock it into the open or closed position as appropriate. You may then have to unscrew the thumb nut on the other side to allow it to pass through any special obstacles on the fork designed to prevent losing the wheel. Tighten the lock-

Spoke tensioning or replacement with nipple wrench.

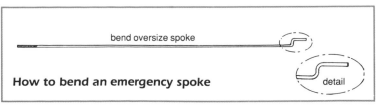

bend oversize spoke

How to bend an emergency spoke

detail

nut again until the use of the lever is effective for locking or unlocking the whole connection.

Replace Broken Spoke

This is the kind of thing that may have to be corrected *en route*. Carry some spokes of the same length and gauge (thickness) used on each wheel and proceed as follows:

1. Remove the old spoke by unthreading it from the old nipple.

2. Find a spoke that is 4 places further over along the rim, or the second spoke over on the same hub flange to use as an example and note how it runs — your spoke must be routed over and under the various spokes it crosses the same way.

3. Install the new spoke and thread it into the nipple using either a nipple wrench or, if you don't have one with you, a small crescent wrench. Tightening it until it has the same tension as other spokes on the same side of the same wheel.

4. Check how well the wheel is trued and correct if necessary following the next procedure.

Note:

If the spoke head is inaccessible, because it lies under the sprockets on the RH side of the rear wheel, you can install a provisional spoke made up as shown in the illustration by bending a longer spoke after the head has been cut off.

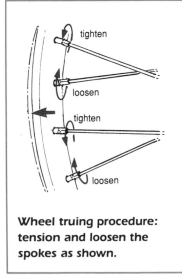

tighten

loosen

tighten

loosen

Wheel truing procedure: tension and loosen the spokes as shown.

Wheel Truing

If the wheel is bent, proceed as follows to straighten it by retensioning certain spokes:

1. Check just where it is off-set to the left, where to the right, by turning it slowly while watching at a fixed reference point, such as the brake shoes. Mark the

Inserting tire lever under the bead of the tire.

"If the hole is very small, so it can't be easily detected, pass the tube slowly past your eye, which is quite sensitive."

relevant sections.

2. Tighten LH spokes in the area where the rim is off-set to the RH side in half-turn steps, while loosening the ones on the LH side — and vice versa.

3. Repeat steps 1 and 2 until the wheel is true enough not to rub on the brakes. This will get you by but, unless you are quite good at it, I suggest you get the job done checked by a bike mechanic as soon as possible.

Fixing a Flat

Even though mountain bike tires are less sensitive than those of most other bikes, sooner or later, every cyclist gets a flat. It helps if you are able to handle this repair yourself. Carry a puncture kit, three tire levers, a pump and perhaps a spare tube. The adhesive quality of the patches in your kit deteriorates over time, so I suggest replacing them once a year. Proceed as follows:

1. Remove the wheel from the bike. On a rear wheel, first select the gear with the small chainwheel and sprocket, then hold the chain with the derailleur back.

2. Check whether the cause is visible from the outside. In that case, remove it and mark its location, so you know where to work.

3. Remove the valve cap and locknut, unscrew the round nut (if you have a Presta valve).

4. Push the valve body in and work one side of the tire into the deeper center of the rim.

5. Put a tire iron under the bead on that side, at some distance from the valve, then use it to lift the bead over the rim edge and hook it on a spoke.

6. Do the same with the second tire iron two spokes to the left and with the third one two spokes over to the right. Now the first one will come loose, so you may use it in a fourth location, if necessary.

7. When enough of the tire sidewall is lifted over the rim, you can lift the rest over by hand.

8. Remove the tube, saving the valve until last, when it must be pushed back through the valve hole.

9. Try inflating and check where air escapes. If the hole is very small, so it can't be easily detected, pass the tube slowly past your eye, which is quite sensitive. If

Put the tire bead back over the rim, making sure the tube is not trapped.

Hold back the derailleur while removing or installing the rear wheel.

still no luck, dip the tube under water, a section at a time: the hole is wherever bubbles escape. Mark its location and dry the tire if appropriate. There may be more than just one hole.

10. Make sure the area around the patch is dry and clean, then roughen it with the sand paper or the scraper from the puncture kit and remove the resulting dust. Treat an area slightly larger than the patch you want to use.

11. Quickly and evenly, spread a thin film of rubber solution on the treated area. Let dry about 3 minutes.

12. Remove the foil backing from the patch, without touching the adhesive side. Place it with the adhesive side down on the treated area, centered on the hole. Apply pressure over the entire patch to improve adhesion.

13. Sprinkle talcum powder from the patch kit over the treated area.

14. Inflate the tube and wait long enough to make sure the repair is carried out properly.

15. Meanwhile, check the inside of the tire and remove any sharp objects that may have caused the puncture. Also make sure no spoke ends project from the rim bed — file flush if necessary and cover with rim tape.

16. Let enough air out of the tube to make it limp but not completely empty. Then reinsert it under the tire, starting at the valve.

17. *With your bare hands*, pull the tire back over the edge of the rim, starting opposite the valve, which must be done last of all. If it seems too tight, work the part already installed deeper into the center of the rim bed, working around towards the valve from both sides.

18. Make sure the tube is not pinched between rim and tire bead anywhere, working and kneading the tire until the tube is free.

19. Install the valve locknut and inflate the tube to about a third its final pressure.

20. Center the tire relative to the rim, making sure it lies evenly all around on both sides.

21. Inflate to its final pressure, then install the wheel. If

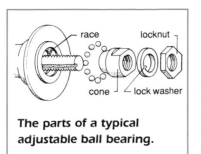

The parts of a typical
adjustable ball bearing.

Loosening the handlebar stem
(above) allows you to pull it
out, revealing the clamping
wedge (below).

the tire is wider than the rim, you may have to
release the brake (just make sure you tighten it again
afterwards). On the rear wheel, refer to point 1 above.

Note:

If the valve leaks, or if the tube is seriously damaged, the
entire tube must be replaced, which is done following
the relevant steps of these same instructions. Replacement of the tire cover is done similarly.

Bearing Adjustment

The ball bearings of the bike, whether used on the hubs,
the pedals, the headset or the bottom bracket all should
be adjusted so that they turn freely and without resistance, yet without discernible lateral play. Check the latter by trying to hold the one part in one hand and a
fixed part on the bike in the other and trying to move the
two sideways relative to each other. If there is any loose-
ness, or if the bearings are so tight that they resist turning freely, adjust them as follows:

1. Undo the locknut with a fitting wrench.
2. Loosen or tighten the underlying cone or cup,
   countering with a second wrench at the opposite side
   or at a fixed point, depending on what kind of bearing it is.
3. Countering at the adjusted cone or cup, tighten the
   locknut again.
4. Check once more and repeat if necessary until
   properly adjusted.

Note:

If you have no luck, it is probably time to have the bike
shop overhaul or replace the entire bearing.

Handlebar Adjustment

The height of the handlebars, as wells their angular
orientation are easy to correct. The only problem is that
in many cases the adjustment of the front brake is affected too, when the handlebars are raised or lowered. If
your front brake cable has its stop or roller on the handlebar stem, rather than on a plate projecting from the

Adjusting saddle angle or forward position.

headset, first loosen the brake and adjust it afterwards.

To adjust the height of the handlebars, loosen the expander bolt on top of the stem. Then lower or raise the bars into the appropriate position, holding it straight there and tighten the expander bolt again.

To adjust the angle of the handlebars, loosen the binder bolts that hold the stem sleeve around the bars and twist the bars into the required orientation while making sure they are exactly centered; then tighten the binder bolts again while holding the handlebars in place.

Saddle Adjustment

Although the height adjustment of the saddle was covered in Chapter 4 and the operation of the quick-release earlier in this chapter, there may be more to it than just adjusting the height alone. To adjust the forward position or the angle of the saddle, first loosen the bolts that hold the saddle's wire frame to the seat post. Then slide it in the desired position and tighten the bolts again.

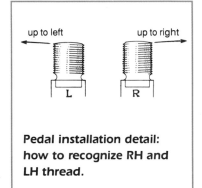

Pedal installation detail: how to recognize RH and LH thread.

Pedal Removal and Installation

Sometimes the pedals have to be removed to transport or store the bike. This is somplicated by the fact that the LH pedal has a special LH screw thread. To establish which pedal goes on the left and which on the right, check for an engraved L or H on the stub that screws into the crank. If they are not marked, consult the illustration to determine yourself which is which.

Most pedals have a recessed hexagon in the end of the stub, so they can be removed or installed with the aid of an Allen key. Looking from the pedal end (rather than from the stub), turn the RH pedal counterclockwise to remove, clockwise to tighten. Again seen from the pedal side, the LH pedsl is turned clockwise to remove, counterclockwise to tighten.

When installing the pedal, carefully match up the thread by hand to prevent cross-threading the stub, which would ruin the screw thread in the rather soft aluminum crank. If you frequently remove the pedals, put some grease on the stub and place a steel washer between the pedal and the crank to protect the crank.

Appendix

Table 1 — Inch gear table (gear number in inches)

	Number of teeth on chainwheel																							
		24	26	28	30	32	34	36	38	39	40	41	42	43	44	45	46	47	48	49	50	51	52	53	
13	48	52	56	60	64	68	72	76	78	80	82	84	86	88	90	92	94	96	98	100	102	104	106	**13**
14	45	48	52	56	60	63	67	70	72	74	76	78	80	82	84	85	87	89	91	93	95	97	98	**14**
15	42	45	49	52	55	59	62	66	68	69	71	73	75	76	78	80	81	83	85	87	88	90	92	**15**
16	39	42	45	49	52	55	58	61	63	65	67	68	70	72	73	75	76	78	80	81	83	85	86	**16**
17	37	40	43	46	49	52	55	58	60	61	63	64	66	67	69	70	72	73	75	76	78	80	81	**17**
18	35	38	40	43	46	49	52	55	56	58	59	61	62	64	65	66	68	69	71	72	74	75	77	**18**
19	33	36	38	41	44	47	49	52	53	55	56	57	59	60	62	63	64	66	67	68	70	71	73	**19**
20	31	34	36	39	42	44	47	49	51	52	53	55	56	57	59	60	61	62	64	65	66	68	69	**20**
21	30	32	35	37	40	42	45	47	48	50	51	52	53	54	56	57	58	59	61	62	63	64	66	**21**
22	28	31	33	35	38	40	43	45	46	47	48	50	51	52	53	54	56	57	58	59	60	61	63	**22**
23	27	29	32	34	36	38	41	43	44	45	46	47	49	50	51	52	53	54	55	57	58	59	60	**23**
24	26	28	30	32	35	37	39	41	42	43	44	45	47	48	49	50	51	52	53	54	55	56	57	**24**
25	25	27	29	31	33	35	37	39	41	42	43	44	45	46	47	48	49	50	51	52	53	54	55	**25**
26	24	26	28	30	32	34	36	38	39	40	41	42	43	44	45	46	47	48	49	50	51	52	53	**26**
27	23	25	27	29	31	33	35	37	38	39	40	41	42	43	44	45	46	47	48	49	50	51	52	**27**
28	22	24	26	28	30	32	33	35	36	37	38	39	40	41	42	43	44	45	46	46	47	48	49	**28**
30	21	23	24	26	28	29	31	33	34	35	36	36	37	38	39	40	41	42	42	43	44	45	46	**30**
32	20	21	23	24	26	28	29	31	32	33	33	34	35	35	37	37	38	39	40	41	41	42	43	**32**
34	18	20	21	23	24	26	28	29	30	31	31	32	33	33	34	35	36	37	37	38	39	40	41	**34**
38	16	18	19	21	22	23	25	26	27	27	28	29	29	30	31	31	32	32	33	34	35	36	36	**38**
		24	26	28	30	32	34	36	38	39	40	41	42	43	44	45	46	47	48	49	50	51	52	53	

Table 2 — Metric gear table (development in meters)

	Number of teeth on chainwheel																							
		24	26	28	30	32	34	36	38	39	40	41	42	43	44	45	46	47	48	49	50	51	52	53	
13	3.80	4.10	4.50	4.80	5.10	5.40	5.70	6.10	6.20	6.40	6.50	6.70	6.90	7.00	7.20	7.30	7.50	7.70	7.80	8.00	8.10	8.30	8.50	**13**
14	3.60	3.90	4.10	4.40	4.70	5.00	5.30	5.60	5.80	5.90	6.10	6.20	6.40	6.50	6.70	6.80	7.00	7.10	7.30	7.40	7.60	7.70	7.90	**14**
15	3.30	3.60	3.90	4.10	4.40	4.70	5.00	5.30	5.40	5.50	5.70	5.80	5.90	6.10	6.20	6.40	6.50	6.60	6.80	6.90	7.10	7.20	7.30	**15**
16	3.10	3.40	3.60	3.90	4.10	4.40	4.70	4.90	5.10	5.20	5.30	5.40	5.60	5.70	5.80	6.00	6.10	6.20	6.40	6.50	6.60	6.70	6.90	**16**
17	2.90	3.20	3.40	3.70	3.90	4.10	4.40	4.60	4.80	4.90	5.00	5.10	5.20	5.40	5.50	5.60	5.70	5.90	6.00	6.10	6.20	6.30	6.50	**17**
18	2.80	3.00	3.20	3.50	3.70	3.90	4.10	4.40	4.50	4.60	4.70	4.80	5.00	5.10	5.20	5.30	5.40	5.50	5.60	5.80	5.90	6.00	6.10	**18**
19	2.60	2.80	3.10	3.30	3.50	3.70	3.90	4.10	4.30	4.40	4.50	4.60	4.70	4.80	4.90	5.00	5.10	5.20	5.40	5.50	5.60	5.70	5.80	**19**
20	2.50	2.70	2.90	3.10	3.30	3.50	3.70	3.90	4.00	4.10	4.30	4.40	4.50	4.70	4.80	4.90	4.90	5.00	5.10	5.20	5.30	5.40	5.50	**20**
21	2.40	2.60	2.80	3.00	3.20	3.40	3.60	3.80	3.90	4.00	4.10	4.20	4.20	4.30	4.40	4.50	4.60	4.70	4.80	4.90	5.00	5.10	5.15	**21**
22	2.30	2.50	2.60	2.80	3.00	3.20	3.40	3.60	3.70	3.80	3.90	4.00	4.10	4.15	4.20	4.30	4.40	4.50	4.60	4.70	4.80	4.90	4.95	**22**
23	2.20	2.30	2.50	2.70	2.90	3.10	3.20	3.40	3.50	3.60	3.70	3.80	3.90	4.00	4.10	4.15	4.20	4.30	4.40	4.50	4.60	4.70	4.80	**23**
24	2.10	2.20	2.40	2.60	2.80	2.90	3.10	3.30	3.40	3.50	3.50	3.60	3.70	3.80	3.90	4.00	4.10	4.15	4.20	4.30	4.40	4.50	4.60	**24**
25	2.00	2.20	2.30	2.50	2.70	2.80	3.00	3.20	3.25	3.30	3.40	3.50	3.60	3.70	3.70	3.80	3.90	4.00	4.10	4.15	4.20	4.30	4.40	**25**
26	1.90	2.10	2.20	2.40	2.60	2.70	2.90	3.00	3.10	3.20	3.30	3.40	3.40	3.50	3.60	3.70	3.80	3.85	3.90	4.00	4.10	4.15	4.20	**26**
27	1.85	2.00	2.20	2.30	2.50	2.60	2.80	2.90	3.00	3.10	3.20	3.25	3.30	3.40	3.50	3.55	3.60	3.70	3.80	3.80	3.90	4.00	4.10	**27**
28	1.80	1.90	2.10	2.20	2.40	2.50	2.70	2.80	2,90	3.00	3.05	3.10	3.20	3.30	3.35	3.40	3.50	3.60	3.65	3.70	3.80	3.90	3.90	**28**
30	1.70	1.80	1.90	2.10	2.20	2.40	2.50	2.60	2.70	2.80	2.90	2.95	3.00	3.05	3.10	3.20	3.30	3.35	3.40	3.50	3.55	3.60	3.70	**30**
32	1.60	1.70	1.80	1.90	2.10	2.20	2.30	2.50	2.55	2.60	2.70	2.75	2.80	2.90	2.95	3.00	3.05	3.10	3.20	3.25	3.30	3.40	3.45	**32**
34	1.50	1.60	1.70	1.80	2.00	2.10	2.20	2.30	2.40	2.45	2.50	2.60	2.60	2.70	2.75	2.80	2.90	2.95	3.00	3.10	3.15	3.20	3.25	**34**
38	1.40	1.50	1.60	1.70	1.80	2.00	2.10	2.20	2.25	2.30	2.40	2.45	2.50	2.55	2.60	2.70	2.75	2.80	2.85	2.90	2.95	3.00	3.10	**38**
		24	26	28	30	32	34	36	38	39	40	41	42	43	44	45	46	47	48	49	50	51	52	53	

The left-side label for both tables reads: **Number of teeth on sprocket**

Table 3 — Frame sizing table (frame size and seat height in inches and cm)

leg length		recommended seat tube height				recommended straddle height ground to top tube	
		A center to top of lug		B center-to-center			
cm	in	cm	in	cm	in	cm	in
73	29	35	14	34		65	26
74		36		35		66	
75		37		35	14	67	
76	30	38	15	36		68	27
77		39		37		69	
78		40		38	15	70	
79	31	41	16	39		71	28
80		42		40	16	72	
81	32	43	17	41		73	29
82		44		42		74	
83		45		43	17	75	
84	33	46	18	44		76	30
85		47		45	18	77	
86	34	48	19	46		78	31
87		49		47		79	
88		50		48	19	80	
89	35	51	20	49		81	32
90		52		50	20	82	
91	36	53	21	51		83	33
92		54		52		84	
93		55		53	21	85	
94	37	56	22	54		86	34
95		57		56		87	

Remarks:

The seat tube lengths shown in this table are recommended values. The maximum size is about one inch (2.5 cm) more, the minimum about one inch (2.5 cm) less.

Index

abrasions, 72
accelerating, 47
access, 12ff
    restrictions, 13f
accessories, 28, 63ff
    for off-season riding, 91f
accident types and how to avoid
them, 66ff
    diverting, 70
    loss of control, 71
    skidding, 70f
    stopping, 70
adjustment,
    of bearings, 121
    of brakes, 114f
    of derailleurs, 115f
    of handlebars, 121
    of saddle, 122
aerobic training, 78ff
altitude, effect of, 89f

back ache, 75
balancing, 42ff, 50f
    while standing still, 50f
bottom bracket, 26
    height, 22
brakes, 11, 27f, 114f
    adjustment and maintenance,
    114
brake types,
    cantilever, 11, 27
    U-brake, 27f
    cam-operated, 27f
brake levers, 28
brake cables, 28
braking technique, 44ff
    for speed control, 46f
    suddenly, 46f
breathing exercises, 82
bronchial complaints, 76

calisthenics, 80f
characteristics of mountain bike,
10ff
chain, 26, 116f
    compatibility with sprockets
    and derailleurs, 26
    maintenance and cleaning,
    116f
    removal and installation, 117
'chain suck,' 66

changer, see derailleur
clearances, of frame, 22
construction methods, of frame,
22
controls, see brakes, gearing
cleaning, of bike, 112f
climbing, 47f
clothing, 17, 61f
    fabrics for, 62
    for bad weather, 62f, 89f
collisions, 69ff
compatibility, of mountain biking
with other activities, 14f
    of chains with sprockets and
derailleurs, 26
competition, also see sport,
racing, 16f, 103ff
    preparation for, 109f
    types of events, 106
components (also parts) 19ff
contour lines, 99f
CO_2 cartridge tire inflator, 64
cranks, 116
cross-chaining, 32

**definition of mountain biking,
12**
    of the mountain bike, 10ff
    of parts of the mountain bike
depressions, 57f
derailleurs, 26f, 30ff, 115f
    controls, 33, 115f
    maintenance and adjustment,
    115f
descending, 48
design of mountain bike, 10f
development, as gear designation,
36
distribution
    of rider's weight, 50
    of luggage 97.
drivetrain, 24ff, 116f
    maintenance, 116f

equipment,
    general, 59ff
    of bike, 62ff
    for racing, 107ff
    for touring, 96
erosion, 14
exercise,

breathing, 82ff
    off-the-bike, 78f
    stretching, 78f

falls, 69
fashion
    in mountain bike clothing, 17f
    in mountain bike design, 18
fenders, 65
fitness, 77ff
    aerobic, 76f
forced turn, 43f
fork, 24
    Koski design, 24
fractures, 72f
frame, 21ff
    design, 22f
    materials, 21f
    tubes, 21f
friction shifting, in derailleur
gearing, 31
front derailleur, see derailleurs

gearing, also see derailleurs,
shifters, 11, 26f, 29ff, 115f
    designation, 35f
    number, see gear designation
    parts, 30
    practice, 37f
    principle, 31f
    progression, 36f
    theory, 33ff
    spread, 35
gloves, 62

handgrips, 23f
handlebars, 10, 23f
    width, 10, 23, 42
    height, 41f
    position, 41f
handlebar stem, see stem
health, 67ff
head injuries, 73
heart rate, 78
helmet, 60, 73
Hite-Rite, 66
hopping, see jumping
hostility against mountain biking,
14f
hubs, 24

index derailleurs, see derailleurs
injuries,
    causes, 69ff
    treatment, 72f
inspection of bike, 113f
integration of components, 11

jumping, 52ff
    sideways, 53f

knee problems, 74

leaning, 43f
leather saddle, 11
lighting equipment, 65
lock, 28, 60
lubrication, 113f
luggage, 97f
luggage racks, 64f, 97f

maintenance, 111ff
    of brake, 114f
    of chain, 116f
    of cranks, 116
    of derailleur, 115f
    of drivetrain, 116f
    of tires, 119f
    of wheels, 117f
maps, 98f
massage, 85f
    procedure, 85f
mudflap, 64
mudguards, see fenders

natural turn, 43f
NORBA, 16, 104f
numbness, 75
    nutrition, for competition, 109f

obstacles,
    jumping across, 55f
off-season cycling, 87f
orientation, 101f

packing luggage, 97f
pedaling rate, 34f
    force, 34f
pedals, 25f
planning,
    of route, 98f, 102
    of tour, 98f

protection,
    against theft, 59f
    of head, 59f
    of other body parts, 60f
pump, 64

quick-release, 10
    operation, 112, 117

racing, see competition
rain,
    clothing, 88f
    riding in, 88f
rear derailleur, see derailleurs
ridges, 56
riding skills, see skills
rims, 24f
risks, 67ff
rough surfaces, 49f
route selection, 99f

saddle, 10f
    adjusting, 41f, 122, 125
    height, 40f
    materials, 11
    position, 41
    quick-release, 10
safety monitoring, 100, 102
sanctioning, of races, 105
scale, of map, 98f
seat post, 10, 122
self-massage, see massage
shifters, 11, 26, 31
    under-the-bar, 11, 27, 31
    above-the-bar, 11, 27, 31
shifting technique, 37f
shock absorption,
    with body, 50
    mechanically, 107
shoes, 63
sinus problems, 76
sizing, 40f, 125
skills
    basic, 39ff
    advanced, 49ff
    for bad weather, 92f
spokes,
    replacement, 118
sprained limbs, 72
starting, 47
steering, 23f, 42ff

steering system, 23f
stem, also handlebar stem, 23,
41f, 122
straddle cable angle, 28
stretching, 80ff
    effects of, 82
sunburn, 76

technique, see skills
tendinitis, 74
theft, 60
    of saddle, 66
tires, 10
    pressure, 10, 25, 64
    size, 10, 24f
    tread, 10, 25
    maintenance, 119f
tool kit, 66
touring, 95ff
traction, 47f, 50f
    when climbing, 48
training,
    for competition, 108f
    for fitness, 78ff
training heart rate, 78f
traffic,
    hazards, 68ff
    riding in, 94
transportation, using the bike for,
94
trials (also observed trials), 16f,
108
turbo trainer, see wind load
simulator
turning techniques, 43f
twist grip shifter, in gearing, 33

U-lock, 57f
UCI, 108
USCF, 16

water bottle, 64
weight distribution, see
distribution
wheels, 24f
    maintenance, 117f
    truing, 117f
wind, effect on riding style, 93
wind chill, 89f
wind load simulator training, 84

Other Books by Bicycle Books

We issue about four new titles each year. The following list is up to date at the time of going to press. If you want more details, you may order our full-color catalog from the address below or by calling (415) 381-2515.

Title	Author	US price
The Mountain Bike Book	Rob van der Plas	$9.95
The Bicycle Repair Book	Rob van der Plas	$8.95
The Bicycle Racing Guide	Rob van der Plas	$9.95
The Bicycle Touring Manual	Rob van der Plas	$9.95
Roadside Bicycle Repairs	Rob van der Plas	$4.95
Major Taylor (hardcover)	Andrew Ritchie	$19.95
Bicycling Fuel	Richard Rafoth	$7.95
In High Gear	Samuel Abt	$10.95
Mountain Bike Maintenance	Rob van der Plas	$7.95
The Bicycle Fitness Book	Rob van der Plas	$7.95
The Bicycle Commuting Book	Rob van der Plas	$7.95
The New Bike Book	Jim Langley	$4.95
Tour of the Forest Bike Race	H.E. Thomson	$9.95
Bicycle Technology	Rob van der Plas	$16.95
Tour de France (hardcover)	Samuel Abt	$22.95
Tour de France (softcover)	Samuel Abt	$12.95
All Terrain Biking	Jim Zarka	$7.95
Mountain Bike Magic	Rob van der Plas	$14.95
The High Performance Heart	Mafetone & Mantell	$9.95

When it comes to buying books, support your local book shop!

To obtain a copy of our current catalog, including full descriptions of all our books, please send your name and address to:
**Bicycle Books, Inc.
PO Box 2038
Mill Valley CA 94941**
or to the national distributor listed on the back cover if you live in Canada or the UK.

We encourage our readers to buy their books at a book or bike shop. Our book trade distributor, The Talman Co., can fill any trade order quickly. They have an 800-number (listed in *Books in Print*) that any book shop can use to order our books. In addition, many bicycle and outdoor sport shops carry our most popular books.

If your local shop is not willing to order the books you want, you can order directly from us. In that case, please include the price of the book plus postage and handling ($2.50 for the first book, $1.00 for each additional book), as well as sales tax for California mailing addresses. When ordering from Bicycle Books, prepayment or credit card number and expiration date are required. We'll gladly fill your order, but we'd prefer you try the book shop first.